THE KING'S NURSERIES

And moreover converted the Monastery of Westminster, a most famous place for the sacring of the Kings of England ... into a Colledgial Church or (as I may better term it) into a seminary of the Church: and there instituted one Dene, 12 Prebends, one Master, one Usher, and Fortie Schollers whom they call the King's Nurseries. And certainly, there come out from thence, happily for Church and Commonwealth, a number of learned Men.

A FOREIGN VISITOR TO WESTMINSTER,
C. 1545

THE KING'S NURSERIES

The Story of Westminster School

JOHN FIELD

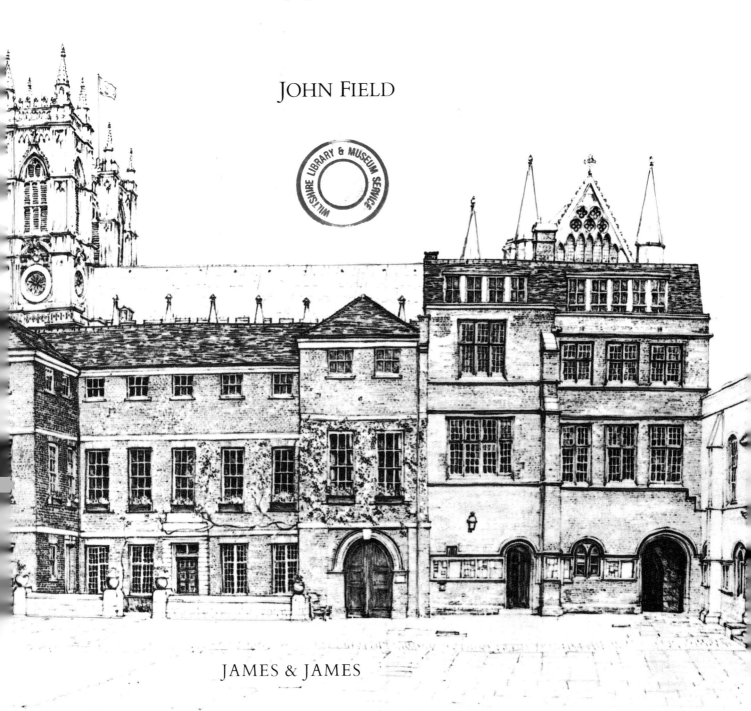

JAMES & JAMES

ACKNOWLEDGEMENTS

I wish to thank all who have helped me in the preparation of this book, especially Enid Nixon and Christine Reynolds in the Westminster Abbey Muniment Room, Sara Stewart for her work on the manuscript, and Ronald Lunt for compiling the index. I acknowledge my indebtedness to previous books about Westminster by F. Markham, F. H. Forshall, John Sargeaunt, Lawrence Tanner and John Carleton, and I am grateful for the friendship and encouragement of Tanner and Carleton in my early years at Westminster. I am also grateful to the Governing Body of the School for giving me the opportunity to write this book, and to individual members of it for their support. But I would emphasize that this is in no sense an 'official' history of the School. The statements made and the views expressed are the responsibility of the author alone.

Colour plates, non-archive photographs and photographs of black and white prints in the main text are all by Malcolm Crowthers. The line drawings on the end papers and jacket are by Francis Burrows. Portraits in the Selected List of Old Westminsters are reproduced by permission of the National Portrait Gallery. Capon's watercolour of Dean's Yard (plates) is reproduced by permission of the Society of Antiquaries.

J.C.D.F. JANUARY 1987

Typeset by V & M Graphics Ltd

Printed in Great Britain by BAS Printers Ltd

Bound by Hunter & Foulis Ltd

Designed by Oliver Hickey

Published by James & James
the registered imprint of Landscape Books Ltd
75 Carleton Road, London N7 0ET

Half title page: Westminster Frolics, a cartoon by Robert Cruickshank, 1823.
Title page: Little Dean's Yard in 1978, from a drawing by John Western.

FOREWORD

by John Rae

Westminster has been fortunate in its historians. School histories are usually bread and butter affairs, the aim of which is to provide a plain chronicle of events which offends no one. Such histories are not inaccurate but they can be dull.

Whatever criticisms may be made of Westminster – and with the exception of Eton, no other English school has provoked such fierce hostility – it cannot be accused of being dull. In this sense the historian's task is made easier; the raw material of an interesting story is already there. But it still requires a skilful hand to do justice both to the colourful incidents and to the less dramatic development of policy and custom.

John Field, like his immediate predecessors Lawrence Tanner and John Carleton, knows and loves the School; and like them he is confident enough of the School's reputation not to confuse a school history with a school prospectus. My impression is that he has been even more fearless than his predecessors in facing the less attractive side of public school life. Skeletons are taken out and observed; vices as well as virtues are recorded.

John Field's text has another important quality: it is not just a re-hash of former versions. He knows the School archives better than anyone and has an eye for the detail that illuminates the attitudes of the period. There is, for example, a particularly telling quotation on the subject of corporal punishment from a boy's diary of the early years of this century.

The sense that John Field's version gives the reader of discovering the School's history afresh is reinforced by his willingness to explore the character and motives of individuals, particularly Head Masters. Previous histories, however scholarly or urbane, were rather reticent on the subject of character. Field chances his arm and his book is more interesting as a result.

These qualities alone would have been ample justification for a new history. But they are really a bonus because the idea behind the project was different. There had never been an *illustrated* history of the School, a strange omission for a place of such visual beauty, eccentric characters and bizarre customs. It was Hamish MacGibbon, an Old Westminster publisher, who proposed that a well illustrated history should be produced which would have the additional merit of bringing the story up to date. John Carleton's history effectively ended with the return of the School to Westminster after the war. The last forty years which have seen such profound changes both in the way schools are run and in the attitudes of parents and pupils, are here described for the first time.

One of the most persistent criticisms of Westminster over the centuries has been that it encourages a certain arrogance in its pupils. There is some justification in that, but it is also true that society has always tended to label as arrogant those men and women who went their own way and exhibited a healthy disrespect for mere convention. Are Westminster boys and girls really as independent minded as this suggests? My reading of this excellent history of the School as well as my experience as Head Master persuades me that many of them are. They are the real heroes of the story. As John Field makes clear, the individualistic or non-conformist tradition, though it may have gone underground at times, is what distinguishes Westminster from the other great schools and remains its most precious possession.

J.M.R. DECEMBER 1986

LIST OF COLOUR PLATES

Plate

1 Queen Elizabeth I   *facing page 32*
   Richard Busby
   Alexander Nowell
   William Camden

2 Little Dean's Yard 1845   *facing page 33*
   Little Dean's Yard 1986

3 School about 1840   *facing page 48*
   College Dormitory about 1840

4 Burlington's Arch 1831   *facing page 49*

5 Little Dean's Yard early nineteenth century   *facing page 64*
   Dean's Yard 1815

6 A metropolitan school –
   a view from Ashburnham House   *facing page 65*
   Ashburnham House staircase
   College Hall – two views

7 College Hall 1816   *facing page 80*
   Westminster from the Victoria Tower

8 Tothill Street in the eighteenth century   *facing page 81*
   Ashburnham House

CONTENTS

Acknowledgements   4

Foreword   *5*

List of colour plates   6

Chapter
  1. Before 1540: Le Sopehous now called the Scolehous   9

  2. His Highnes Scole: 1540–1603   17

  3. Gloves for Mr Busby: 1603–1695   31

  4. Polite Young Ruffians: 1695–1803   45

  5. Ready to Fight Everybody: 1803–1919   61

  6. Zeal for a Crisis: 1919–1945   83

  7. Dear Liberated One: 1945–1986   97

  8. The School Buildings   113

  9. Selected List of Old Westminsters   129

  10. Chronology   140

Index   143

TO MY WESTMINSTER FRIENDS

It will never be well with the nation until
Westminster School is suppressed.

RICHARD OWEN
Dean of Christ Church 1650–59

Geniuses and boobies have been brought up in it,
who would have been geniuses and boobies had they been
brought up anywhere else.

GEORGE COLMAN, 1772

Eton boatmen,

   Harrow gentlemen,

Westminster scoundrels,

   Winchester scholars.

NINETEENTH CENTURY RHYME

1

BEFORE 1540:

LE SOPEHOUS NOW CALLED THE SCOLEHOUS

FORTUNE, goddess of rogues and comedy, has as much claim as St Peter to be the patron saint of Westminster School. The story to be told is rich in the ebb and flow of favour and disfavour, fashion and neglect. Accident far more than design has determined the School's changing character, its metamorphoses, its very survival. Anyone reading these pages who has any responsibility for this or any similar institution should take heart: in the perspective of history, no human decisions, however critical they appear, are of much consequence beside the haphazard stumbling along from year to year which seems to become the bloodstream of ancient foundations.

Reason and nature, twin props of enlightenment, would aver, on the evidence, that Westminster should by now be extinct. A monastic school which survived the Reformation; a royalist school which survived the Commonwealth; a city school which survived the Industrial Revolution; a church school which survived ecclesiastical meanness and neglect; a boarding school which has retained its residential community despite confident predictions of its disappearance for over a hundred years; a wartime school which survived five years' dissociation from its roots, the destruction of its vital buildings, and desperate poverty. All public schools have shown great powers of self-preservation when their continuance has been threatened. Westminster's have been extraordinary. Like forms of life which

Top hats and tail coats (*left*) photographed in the 1930s and the monastic-style gown shown in the Ackermann print (*right*) which was worn until the 1840s.

thrive when attacked, Westminster seems to have been stimulated by crises to an adaptation tenaciously biological in character.

The waves of time imprint across the centuries patterns, often ironical, that also seem to be organic laws. Moving from town to country was part of the annual rhythm in the sixteenth and seventeenth centuries, when a house at Chiswick offered refuge from plague in late summer and early autumn. The recession of plague anchored the school again in Westminster during the eighteenth century, but rural longings persisted and there were continual rumours of a new site. In the 1840s, Head Master Liddell and Prince Albert went riding together to prospect sites and a move was aired once more in the 1860s. Three eventual moves to the country in successive years, 1938, 1939 and 1940, were enforced and largely unprepared, and for several months the school resembled a nomadic tribe more than an academic institution. Evacuation in Herefordshire and ruins in Westminster prompted the last serious talk of removal in 1945. It is tempting to presume that there will be no more, but the lesson of history is that our presumption may be over-bold.

There is a law of dress too. The monastic gowns we first find costed in the Almoner's accounts of the fourteenth century continued to be worn long after monastic life had disappeared, indeed, into the nineteenth century, if we are to believe the Ackermann print of the Westminster Scholar. Knee breeches and stockings were worn until the 1840s, long after they had ceased to be fashionable wear for gentlemen and had become the livery of servants. In Pickwick Papers (1836–8) Dickens comments that the waiters in the White Hart at Bath 'in their knee breeches looked like Westminster boys, but the illusion was soon dispelled by their better behaviour'. Top hats, tail coats and wing collars which replaced them prevailed until 1939, by which year they were largely picturesque incongruities. And now even to insist that teenagers wear grey suits seems an anachronism. Perhaps blue jeans will survive in the future only in institutions that make a habit of living at least one step behind the fashion.

So chequered a history makes public ignorance about Westminster compared with, say, Eton and Harrow, not altogether surprising. Even knowledgeable Londoners are seldom sure where it is. It doesn't look like a school, even when its inhabitants are on view if it is the end of the formal day and suits have been discarded. So it is entirely in character that not much is known about its origins.

A monastic school, with birch rod prominent. A woodcut from Johannes de Garlandia's *Synonima* printed in London in 1502, from the Busby Library. The length of the boys' hair is notable, and was not matched until the early 1970s.

The eleventh century stone vault in 'The Dungeons': the Undercroft of the monastic Rere-Dorter. The roof still carries the marks of the wooden shuttering which supported mortar and rubble while it set. The room has been used in its time as a monastic prison and kitchen, the wine cellar for Ashburnham House, a store for the Latin Play scenery, and, after partitioning, as a set of music practice rooms.

The roof of College Hall, probably by Hugh Herland, the carpenter who also constructed the roof of Westminster Hall. College Hall was completed in about 1375. The recess in the central section of the roof originally contained louvres for the release of the smoke from a raised central fireplace. This medieval practice survived here until 1846. The wooden porch of College Hall (*right*) in the courtyard of the Deanery, formerly the Abbot's House, a fortified residence completed in the fourteenth century.

All that can be said for certain is that Westminster is a medieval school of monastic foundation. Yet the precise moment at which a grammar school for boys became separately identifiable from the monastic institution of novices and from the provisions made for singing boys is likely to remain undefined. But there is no doubt that medieval practices, persisting down the centuries, have had a large share in determining the character of the school. The monastic community, its rules and its scholarly links with the universities decided the form in which it was redefined twice in the mid-sixteenth century, first by Henry VIII in 1540 and again by Elizabeth I in 1560. The Challenge, an oral grammatical contest for admission to College as a Scholar, prolonged over many weeks, is clearly a kind of medieval disputation observed by William Fitzstephen in the twelfth century, again by John Stow in the sixteenth, and survived largely unchanged until the nineteenth. The Latin Play, which lasted as a December festivity until 1938, was the direct descendant of the monastic practice of presenting before the Abbot Christmas plays and entertainments first recorded in 1413, and expressly commanded in the Elizabethan Statutes of 1560. The Shrove Tuesday Pancake Greaze, which still continues, though not recorded historically before the mid-eighteenth century, must have had its roots in medieval custom.

Physically no less than historically Westminster is an archeological site resembling a palimpsest: post-war, pre-war, Victorian, eighteenth century,

Opposite. Layers of medieval work seen from the roof of Ashburnham House. At the bottom of the picture is the twelfth century arcading of the refectory. Above it are the blind windows of the cloister rebuilt by Abbot Litlyngton in the fourteenth century, and behind them the thirteenth century lines of Henry III's Abbey, completed in the fifteenth century when the romanesque nave was finally replaced by Gothic. The work in progress is the replacement of unsound nineteenth century stonework.

Stuart, Tudor, medieval Westminster are all layered one on another and one beside another; all the layers are visible, and the first layer is always monastic. The eleventh century is there in the Undercroft of the monastic Rere-Dorter, rechristened the Dungeons, and now used for plays, recitals, lectures and parties. Eleventh century also are parts of the south and west walls of School, the Hall once used as the Dormitory of the Benedictine Monastery, and two external windows of that original dormitory with their Norman decoration, one incongruously located behind a blackboard in a modern classroom. There are both Saxon cobbles and twelfth century arcading in Ashburnham Garden, once the monastic Refectory, now a peaceful and melancholy green shade between the School and the Abbey. There are thirteenth century windows at the north end of School, and on the ground floor of Ashburnham House, where subsequent builders saw no point in removing the massive outer walls of the Prior's Lodging. College Hall, where the central fire that burned in many medieval great halls remained in use until the 1840s, was Abbot Litlyngton's State Dining Room of the late fourteenth century, and is used now as the school's principal dining hall, as it was in 1540 and has been ever since. The senior members of the Collegiate body, the Dean and Canons, who joined the corporate meals in the early days, withdrew to the greater comforts of their own residences during the seventeenth century and left the place to the Scholars and, more recently, the 'Town Boys' and girls of an expanding school.

In the early centuries, however, there was no more than a handful of pupils. The scanty statistical information in the Almoner's accounts gives us a total of thirteen boys in 1370, twenty-eight boys in 1385. A doubling of the schoolmaster's annual stipend from 13s. 4d. to 26s. 8d in 1395, and a further increase to 40s. in 1480 may be related to increasing numbers, for the stipend of the Master of the Singing Boys seems to have remained at 13s. 4d. at these times. It is not an unreasonable surmise that the provision for forty Scholars in the 1540 Statutes reflects continuity rather than change.

The evidence for the foundation of this small one-room grammar school is indeterminate. The Benedictine monastery of Westminster was, in comparison with other great houses, of late foundation, probably in the tenth century, and was of no special consequence until Edward the Confessor's building of the Romanesque church depicted as incomplete in the Bayeux Tapestry. The now discredited Chronicle of Ingulphus, Monk of Croyland, narrates a fairy-tale encounter between himself as a boy and Edith, the Confessor's Queen, engaging in grammatical repartee in their leisure moments. More trustworthy, but alas, unspecific, is Fitzstephen's *Chronicle History of St Thomas*. In his account of London in the reign of Henry II, he records that the boys of the schools attached to the three chief churches 'wrangle with one another in verse, contending about the principles of grammar, or the perfect tense or supines'. He also notes the psychologically more plausible feature of 'scoffs and sarcasms against their schoolmasters touching the foibles of their schoolfellows, or perhaps of greater personages'. St Clement's Well by Temple Bar was the favoured site for such encounters 'when on a summer's evening they are disposed to take an airing'.

The similarity between this description and Stow's in his *Survey of London* is some evidence for a continuing tradition of inter-school academic matches in which Westminster boys were involved:

> I myself, in my youth, have yearly seen, on the eve of St Bartholemew the Apostle, the scholars of divers grammar schools repair to the churchyard of St Bartholemew where some one scholar hath stepped up, and there opposed and answered, till he were of some better scholar overcome and put down; and then the overcomer, taking his place, did like as the first, and in the end the best opposer and answerer had rewards . . . I remember there repaired to these exercises the master and scholars of St Paul's, London, and St Peter's, Westminster.

In 1179, Pope Alexander III decreed that some monasteries were to conduct a school, in terms which suggested that others already had one. It would be surprising if twelfth century Westminster were in neither category. Although the carved grids of nine holes for the game of Nine Men's Morris in the stone benches in the North West Cloister where instruction took place suggest the furtive pas-times of bored novices, they proclaim 'schoolboy' across the centuries. A set of rules for schoolboys from the thirteenth century survives in the Abbey records. Twelve of the fifteen injunctions prescribe the birch, and the long list of what boys should not do is a valuable documentary record of daily life.

The unchanging schoolboy: holes scored by coins in the modern brickwork of the School Store by boys waiting in the queue; (*inset*) holes scored in the stone benches of the Cloister by monastic novices for the medieval game of Nine Men's Morris.

No laughing, talking, giggling or smirking if someone reads or intones poorly. No open or surreptitious scuffling, and don't answer back if asked to do something . . . whoever presumes to speak in English or French in reply to Latin, be it with friend or cleric, let him endure a stroke for any word . . . if dice are found in anyone's hand, let him feel a birch blow on naked flesh for each point.

The birch groves of England must have been rapidly denuded. In the fourteenth century, the evidence accumulates. A boy's keep in the Almonry is recorded in the accounts for 1318, and in 1339 9s. 8d. from the Chamberlain's accounts 'for one such' is paid to John Payne for finding Scholars for the School, in what appears to be an early example of head-hunting. In 1373 there are items for the purchase of bread for the master and elementary pupils, and for his tonsure (xvid). By 1386 he has become 'magistro grammatic' and by 1394 'magistro scolarum pro erudicione puerorum'. We learn the names of some of the early schoolmasters from the legal disputes in which they were involved: George Mortymer in Chancery; John Newborough, fined 8d. in 1427 'for owning a gutter going out of his dwelling to the great annoyance of those crossing Thieving Lane'; William Baker, fined iiis. iiiid. at a frankpledge in 1494 for insulting and striking a blow at Thomas Kyrkeham. The 'Scolehouse' is first mentioned in the accounts in 1443–4, though in 1446 we also find 'Le Sopehous now called the Scolehous'. In 1461 it seems the School moved from the Almonry, opposite the west end of the Abbey, into a room in the Steward's and Cellarer's ranges on the east side of Dean's Yard, and so put down its roots on the site it still occupies over five hundred years later. The best interpretation of this varied evidence, and one which pre-empts wrangling, would be that at the time of Henry VIII's de-monasticising of the School in 1540, it had already had continuous existence as a charitable grammar school for over 200 years, and perhaps much longer.

The first list of Scholars and Schoolmasters from the Henry VII Statutes of 1541 or 1542: 39 Scholars, John Adams, Schoolmaster of the Grammar School, and Odnell Hebbone, Usher of the same School.

2

HIS HIGHNES SCOLE:
1540—1603

BEFORE 1540, the school seldom numbered more than twenty boys in a monastic community which, at its height, may have contained over three hundred people. Its function was primarily charitable, though it may also have supplied novices for the monastic order. The school as we know it was born in the Reformation. Henry VIII's challenge to Rome, the dissolution of the monasteries and his assumption of the title of Defender of the Faith changed the Benedictine Abbey of St Peter into the College of St Peter. The school remained an organic part of the foundation (and, of course, continued so until 1868), but its status was immeasurably advanced by royal patronage and by an academic curriculum which placed it, for the first time, on the same footing as Eton and Winchester.

The King's general model for the Bishoprics that were to replace the dissolved abbeys was collegiate and emphatically academic. Though the five readers prescribed were in both humanity and divinity, the range of subjects to be taught (Greek, Hebrew, Latin, Civile and Physike) would appear to make state rather than church the beneficiary. A Bishop, as President of the College, twelve Prebendaries, sixty scholars 'to be taughte both grammar and logik in Hebrue, Greke and Latten', a Schoolmaster and an Usher, and twenty students in divinity, ten at Oxford and ten at Cambridge, completed the Collegiate body.

The book of 'the King's new College at Westminster' dated 17th December

1541, matches the model in all essential respects, but lists only thirty-nine Scholars. John Adams is named Schoolmaster and Odnell Hebbone is Usher. Not all the changes, it seems, were as total as the word 'dissolution' suggests. William Boston, formerly Abbot, is named Dean, and the emphasis on divinity students at Oxford and Cambridge seems only to confirm the established practice of the Benedictine house at Westminster. Four of these twenty are identified as former monks. The King completed his establishment in 1543 by endowing the church with 'divers lands'. What Thomas Cranmer and Sir Anthony Denny, in letters of the 1540s to the Dean and Chapter, call 'The King's Grammar School' and 'His highnes scole', seems, for the next twenty years, the most stable element in a volatile College. For in 1550 the Bishopric was suppressed, and its estates, rights and privileges confirmed the next year on the Dean and Chapter alone. By 1553, at Mary's accession, the 'grammar children' of monastic days had already acquired the title 'King's Scholars'. Accounts and leases in the Abbey Muniment Room provide strong evidence for the continuity of the School throughout the decade from 1550 to 1560. The brief restoration of the monastery (1556–8) appears to have had no effect on the running of the school. The admission lists from 1542 to 1556 reveal a steady complement of Scholars (between thirty-eight and forty-two) each receiving a yearly wage or stipend of 66/8d., and a waiting list, for between 1547 and 1554 there are admissions on thirty-two separate dates as vacancies occurred. The large proportion of boys admitted 'in his brother's place' suggests that the charitable basis of the monastic school was perpetuated in the new foundation. It seems, from an account of the admission procedure of 1545, that the Dean and twelve Prebendaries were to divide the nomination of Scholars between them, such appointments being always referred to as 'gifts' or 'lots'. Two safeguards against abuse are instituted: all children nominated are to be brought before the Dean and the Schoolmaster for the assessment of their suitability; any Prebendary who is proved to have received reward for his nominations is to lose his right of nomination for ever. Possibly the pressures for admission had tempted some to corruption. In 1546 the Dean and Chapter conceded the right of some Scholars to lodge at home or with their friends: the flexibility and diversity of the School's domestic arrangements were thus established early in its life.

John Adams, the first Master of the new School, was quickly replaced by Alexander Nowell, a distinguished scholar who founded the study of Anglo-Saxon England. He was also a celebrated fisherman and, according to Thomas Fuller, accidentally invented bottled beer when he left his picnic ale one day at his riverside retreat at Hadham in Hertfordshire, and returned to find it effervescent. Nowell presided over the School from 1542 to at least 1553, and introduced the study of Terence. During Mary I's reign, he fled to the Continent to escape the stake, but later returned to hold high office at St Paul's and Windsor, to write the short and longer catechisms, and to live, a remarkable survivor, until 1602, when he was ninety-five.

In 1555 Nicholas Udall, author of *Ralph Roister Doister*, the earliest surviving English comedy, was admitted to be Schoolmaster. He had been appointed Head Master of Eton in 1534, and there introduced performances of plays by Plautus

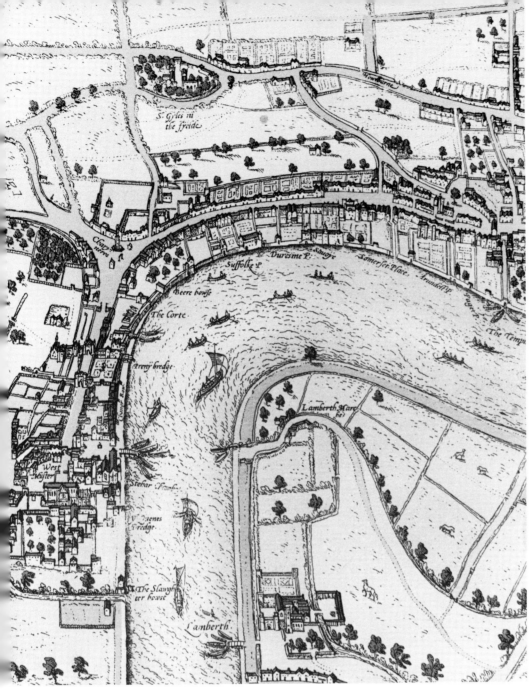

and Terence. He was dismissed in 1541 for pederasty and imprisoned in the Marshalsea, but regained ecclesiastical favour after 1547. His record was evidently no barrier to his return to school life. His tenure was short, however; he was buried in St Margaret's in December 1556. Throughout this period the Schoolmaster's salary remained at its pre-Reformation level, £20 per annum. A Chapter decree of 1555, naming 12 pence as the fixed fine for any of the petty canons, schoolmasters or clerks above the age of eighteen calling any of the Prebendaries 'foole, knave, or any other contumelius or slanderous worde' is a significant financial deterrent for vulgar disrespect towards the hierarchy. No doubt these were contentious years, though all colleges, academic and ecclesiastical, seem to spawn contention as a necessary law of their being even in tranquil times.

Westminster, Whitehall, and Lambeth in 1560, from a contemporary map.

19

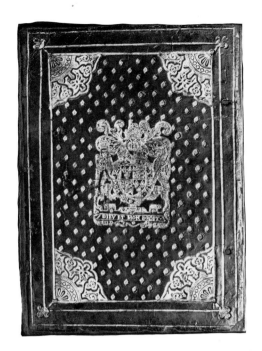
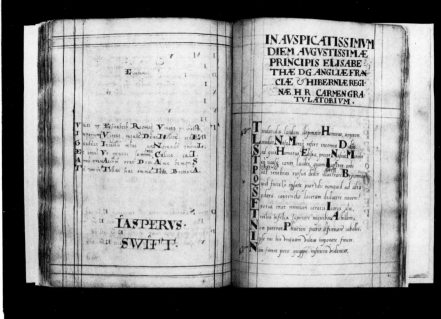

The volume of poems presented to Elizabeth I by the Queen's Scholars in 1587: the binding with the royal coat of arms (*left*), and a double page showing Jasper Swift's skill at acrostics (*right*).

May 21st 1560 is the date of the letters patent conferring a charter upon the Abbey Church. There is no evidence that the subsequent Statutes were ever signed and sealed. Several draft versions exist, though none can with certainty be dated earlier than 1567. However, in all subsequent disputes, the power of custom has always been held to over-ride doubts about their legal status. These Statutes, extensive and detailed, establish a structure and curriculum which was to prevail with largely unquestioned authority for about three hundred years. They also give us the clearest possible view of the aims of Tudor education, and go a long way towards explaining why the memory of Elizabeth I as foundress has entirely ousted that of her father.

It seems, from the frequency of her visits to the School, that Elizabeth took an unusually personal interest in its affairs. She commanded that Maundy, £2 a year, should be distributed for good work, and she attended plays. There survive, at Hatfield and Westminster, handsomely bound copies of Latin and Greek poems presented to her by Westminster Scholars, probably on her New Year visits in 1586 and 1587. In addition, the whole College and not only the School, seems to have felt relief and gratitude for its release from years of confusion. Well into the nineteenth century, the Abbey bells were still being rung every November 17th, 'the day of Queen Elizabeth our Foundress', or Foundation Day.

The rationale of Elizabeth's School is manifest in the 1560 charter, that 'the youth which is growing to manhood, as tender shoots in the wood of our state, shall be liberally instructed in good books to the greater honour of the state'. The detailed prescriptions for the School which embody this aim are, in all likelihood, the work of two successive Deans of Westminster, William Bill (1560–61) and Gabriel Goodman (1561–1601). Bill was also Provost of Eton, and Eton's Statutes must have been open before the compiler of Westminster's. The prescriptions for the day's activities follow Eton's to the letter, beginning with the call of 'Surgite' at five o'clock, through the routines of prayers, cleaning, washing and processing to the Schoolroom at six. Likewise the sequence of academic tests exactly

Opposite. Tudor Westminster: two Ushers' chairs of the 1520s, a blackjack or leather jug used for the Scholars' beer brewed in the College Brewhouse, and the fireplace of Sir John Fortescue's house of 1596, a rebuilding of the Prior's house. Medieval and Elizabethan features were both incorporated into the ground floor of Ashburnham House in 1662–5.

duplicates Eton's, even down to the details of the appointment of a 'custos', or dunce, in each form, and the feature of the Fourth Form's oscillating between Lower Master and Head Master. The authors prescribed for study at Westminster follow closely the Etonian sequence: Vives and Cato in the first form; Terence, Aesop and Cicero in the second and third forms; Ovid's *Tristia* and *Metamorphoses*, Cicero's de *Amicitia*, Caesar's *Commentaries*, and Virgil in the higher forms.

From the outset, different types of pupil are identified: Scholars, Pensioners, Peregrines and Oppidans. Scholars were the only pupils recognised as belonging to the Collegiate body. Their education was free, and they were required to reside in a dormitory provided for them in the precincts, and take their meals in College Hall with the Dean, Prebendaries and other College officers. Pensioners were boys who boarded with the Dean, Prebendaries or Schoolmasters and as full-time residents of the precinct were bound by the same laws as the Scholars. Peregrines were boys from the shires who resided in term time with relatives or friends; Oppidans lived in their own homes. The complement of the School was set at a maximum of one hundred and twenty; Scholars and Pensioners alike were required within fifteen days to find a tutor to supervise their health, bed-linen and moral well-being, as a condition of being admitted to commons, the meals shared by the whole College.

From 1560 an annual ceremony called the Election shaped the destinies of the School and its pupils. It was a public event which combined solemnity, ritual and festivity, and which remained the hub of the yearly cycle of school life until after the Second World War. Three days were set aside for oral examinations which served a triple function: the admission of boys into the School, the election of 'minor candidates' as Scholars and members of the Collegiate body, and the election of 'major candidates', boys at the end of their schooldays, to Christ Church, Oxford and Trinity College, Cambridge. Elizabeth I had required that at least six Westminster pupils should be admitted annually to these two colleges. Though there is abundant evidence in the frequency of disputes in subsequent centuries that Christ Church and Trinity have not always been grateful for Her Majesty's command, closed scholarships continued to be awarded to Westminsters until the 1970s, and the Dean of Christ Church and Master of Trinity not only had a leading voice in the selection of Head Masters of Westminster, but still remain ex officio members of the Governing Body. Until the end of the nineteenth century, election to Christ Church and Trinity was restricted to Westminster Scholars. So the election of 'minor candidates' had an importance which extended way beyond school days. Therefore the innovation introduced in the 1560 Statutes, that all those chosen as Scholars must have been in the School for at least a year before their election, was a crucial one: all boys began as 'Town Boys', and the competitiveness generated between them for the potentially lifelong rewards of the election was the heart of a thriving school.

Seven electors, representing Westminster and the two university Colleges, met on the Monday after SS. Peter and Paul, to set academic exercises to 'those in the highest class who most excel in learning'; to assess in the minor candidates the qualities of gentleness of disposition, ability, learning, good character and poverty; to test the basic literacy of any boy under the age of eight seeking admission to the School; ability to write his own name, parentage and town, and knowledge by heart of the eight parts of speech. No boy was to be elected Scholar if he had expectations of more than £10 a year as his inheritance: this charitable condition was the ladder by which such Scholars as Richard Neile, son of a tallow chandler, rose to become Archbishop of York, and Ben Jonson, stepson of a bricklayer, the most learned poet of his time. The insistence on an ostensibly competitive entry to scholarships, rather than one in which Dean and Prebendaries nominated boys, made Westminster unique among the great schools until the mid-nineteenth century.

The office of the two Schoolmasters sounds, in its description, impossibly exacting. 'Piety, learning, honesty and conscientiousness' were merely foundations for duties academic and pastoral ranging from the teaching of Hebrew grammar to inspection for lice. The longest section of the Statutes prescribes the instruction and discipline of the Scholars. Between rising at five and going to bed at eight, eleven hours of study had to be endured, relieved only by three hours for meals, at eight, eleven, and six, and the very first hour of the day, which was for washing and cleaning. Prayers were said on six occasions during the day; the Latin forms laid down in 1560 are still spoken at Grace in College Hall at lunchtime; and in the Lord's prayer, versicles and responses still sung by the whole School each week at Latin Prayers. During lunch and dinner the monastic practice of readings in Latin from manuscript Old and New Testaments survived.

The Schoolroom was divided. The lower three classes were principally the Second Master's or Usher's responsibility, the upper three the Head Master's, and the fourth form alternated between them. The Usher's duties began at 6.00 a.m.; the Head Master was allowed another hour in bed. Of the eleven hours devoted to study, two were supervised by monitors, older boys who had specific teaching responsibilities. The activities of the rest of the day included the testing of grammar, repetition of passages from memory, translation, prose and verse composition both from given passages and on set themes, the exposition of authors by the masters, and the extraction by the boys of 'expressions, phrases, terms of speech, antitheses, epithets, synonyms, proverbs, likeness, comparisons, narratives, descriptions of time, place and persons, fables, bons mots, schemes and apothegms'. The weariness of this routine was recognised: a boy could formally obtain permission to 'dor' – to drop his head on his hand for sleep. All proceedings in the Schoolroom had to be in Latin, and speaking English there was punishable. Vigilance for error was sharpened by the appointment of a scapegoat, or 'custos' in each form, who was always the first to be called in oral testing. This exposed position was transferred to another if he either spoke English, or proved unable to repeat a rule with fewer than four mistakes, or made three spelling mistakes in his book.

The inexorable pattern of these days, rendered still more remorseless by stretching out over forty-six weeks every year, was marginally relieved by games (but only in an afternoon, not more than once a week, and not in weeks containing a feast day), and music (one hour on Wednesdays and Fridays, instructed by the Master of the Choristers). Towards the end of a week too there was a perceptible

College House, the refuge from city plagues acquired by Dean Goodman in 1570 and used regularly by the School, usually from July to late autumn, until the early eighteenth century. It continued as a country residence for Prebendaries and Head Masters until the 1760s, and was demolished in about 1870.

lightening. Fridays were set aside for revision and repetition of the week's work, preceded by the charging of those who had committed serious offences.

On Sundays and feast days, one hour in the morning was given over to study of the catechism and the learning of the scriptures, and in the afternoon, versions of the sermon preached in the morning were demanded, in English, from the lower forms, Latin from the middle forms, and Greek from the higher forms.

The Scholars, dressed in 'sad-coloured gowns of London russet', and Pensioners were not allowed to leave the precinct, but nor were the Schoolmasters without the Dean's permission. Further evidence here, maybe, of the pervasiveness of the monastic spirit. Scholars were never to depart from the company of their fellows, on pain of flogging, and lost their place absolutely if absent for more than twenty days in a year.

Institutionalised absenteeism, sometimes for several months at a time, was enforced on the whole School soon after its refoundation. The visitations of plague in most years from mid-summer to late autumn threatened communal life in the city. In 1563, the College horse is specially shod to assist the first recorded dispersion to a private house at Putney, where the School stayed some weeks. Other removals in the 1560s were to Wimbledon and Wheathampstead, but in 1570 a permanent retreat was established. One pluralism had brought Eton's curriculum to Westminster, another took Westminster to Chiswick. Dean Goodman, also prebend of Chiswick, obtained a tenancy in perpetuity of the prebendal estate and ordered the enlargement of the Mansion house for the lodging of one of the prebendaries, Schoolmaster, Usher and 40 children of the grammar school. It was 'a place convenient in the country whereunto the youth of the Grammer scole of Westminster may resorte and be instructed in good literature with little losse of time as may be in time of sickness'. As often as not for the next hundred years we hear of the School's decamping in July, usually until October and sometimes until Christmas. Boats and carts were hired to carry beds and books up river for an extended and presumably more leisured academic routine that looks back to *The Decameron* and forward to college reading parties. Though there is little evidence of school use after 1700, memories of Chiswick must have been strong enough for the name to be transferred in the eighteenth century to the sick room in Grants, the oldest school boarding house, and where 'Chiswicks' still persists in the geography of the place. The old house at Chiswick survived until the 1870s; its basically medieval walls gave the demolishers much trouble.

The final paragraph of the section of the Statutes called 'Instruction and Discipline' is headed 'Comedies and Plays at Christmas'. 'In order that the boys may celebrate Christmastide with greater benefit' the masters are instructed, on pain of a fine of ten shillings for their negligence, to provide for the performance of a comedy or tragedy in Latin. The Christmas theatrical tradition certainly had medieval origins. In 1413 there is a reference to boys playing before the Abbot at Christmas, and in 1462 an item in the accounts records the lavish sum of £9. 6s. 8d. for the dressing of the elementary boys for the feast of St Nicholas, and a reference in 1569 to 'the charge of the shewe at paedonomus the children's lorde his creation', suggests that the much older practice of the saturnalian reversal of roles, as in the feast of the Boy Bishop, survived the Reformation. In 1564 two plays, *Miles Gloriosus* by Plautus and *Heautontimoroumenos* by Terence were acted before the Queen. The innovation became an instant tradition, for there are frequent references to plays and their expenses right through to the end of the reign, many played before the Queen or the Council, and extending from Christmas through to Shrovetide. It is chiefly from these accounts that we catch a less formal glimpse of School life in the sixteenth century, for which little documentary evidence survives.

> For buttered beer for ye children, being horse . . . for paper for them to wright out their partes . . . aquavitae and sugar candee for the children . . . or colors and golde foyle bestowed in colouring the children's faces . . . given to a painter for drawing the temple of Jerusalem and for paynting townes . . . for a bagpype plaier . . . for the lone of a throndre barrell and to two men which brought the same and thondred . . . for the bynding of one copie in vellume with the Queen's Majesties armes and sylke ribben stringes.

The passion for theatre seems to have taken strong hold at Westminster; Ben Jonson is perhaps recalling his own experiences, as well as echoing Hamlet's implied strictures on the 'aery of children', when in *The Staple of News* he has his allegorical character, Censure, complain

The gallery in College Hall was added in the second half of the sixteenth century, and the earliest Latin Plays were performed in front of it for Elizabeth and her Council. The tables on the extreme left and right of the picture are of the same period.

> They make all their scholars play-boys. Is't not a fine sight to see all our children made interluders? Do we pay our money for this? We send them to learn their grammar and their Terence, and they learn their play books.

Many a subsequent parent must have made the same rueful protest, for the gift of performance seems to have been bestowed on the School in its cradle. On Saturdays after lunch, declamations on a given theme would be made by two or three Scholars, publicly in College Hall before the whole College. Scholars elected to Oxford and Cambridge were required to deliver valedictory orations before the whole School. As early as 1564, it seems, the Election was followed by a dinner at which the entertainment was provided in the form of verses and epigrams by the successful candidates. The Election Dinner was later to become a celebrated event. Jonathan Swift was scornful of the formal proceedings of the Election in 1711, but looked forward to joining the Election Dinner:

> I was at the Election of lads at Westminster today, and a very silly thing it is; but they say there will be fine doing tomorrow . . . . Mr. Harley is to hear the Elections tomorrow, and we are all to dine and hear fine speeches.

26

The vanity of human wishes! His journal for the next day records:

> I was balked at Westminster; I came too late. I heard no speeches or verses. They
> would not let me in to their dining place for want of a ticket, and I would not send in
> for one, because Mr. Harley excused his coming and Atterbury was not there; and I
> cared not for the rest.

Though the academic ceremonies have disappeared, largely because of changes in university admission procedure, their festive accompaniment, the Election Dinner, still concludes the school year, and still attracts public men: in recent years Enoch Powell and Lord Hailsham have both contributed their own extempore epigrams.

There was an intrinsic theatricality, too, about even the routines of schooling when all the forms were taught together in a single room. This practice lasted from the earliest times to 1883. The growth of the School under Grant and Camden compelled a move, in 1599, from the Cellarer's building in Dean's Yard, to the empty monastic dormitory on the south side of the Abbey, and on the same axis as the transepts of the church. Here in this high narrow echoing hall, below the oak hammerbeam roof, daily life acquired its own dramatic rituals. The rules of 1630 require a pupil who is to recite from memory or talk off the cuff on a given theme to advance into the middle, stand straight, with face up and feet together, and pronounce the words with a clear and distinct voice without any hesitation or stuttering. Punishments too were public affairs. When a boy was sent up to the Head Master, a junior Scholar was appointed to fetch one of the birch rods projecting, handle first, from the rod drawer of the table. He was not allowed to touch it directly but had to grasp it with the sleeve of his gown, as if it were a sacred object. Once the strokes had been given, the Head Master would fling the rod away across the floor of the room to be retrieved and replaced by the same Scholar in the same deferential manner. Proceedings 'Up School' were of unfailing interest to visitors who came to Westminster for entertainment much as in later periods they patronised Bedlam or the London Zoo. In the seventeeth century 'plump-walkers' or fashionable young men of the town came not only to witness the cleverness and ingenuity of the Scholars, but also to engage with them in academic repartee. Access to Law Courts, when they were grouped around Westminster Hall, and to Parliament, a privilege still retained by the Queen's Scholars, as well as to the theatres of the town, has always been regarded as a natural and proper extensions of a Westminster schooling. From Judge Jeffreys to Sir Michael Havers, from Ben Jonson to Sir John Gielgud, the pull of the histrionic professions has been powerful and continuous.

The Queen's favour and the long periods of office of Goodman as Dean and Edward Grant and William Camden as Schoolmasters won for the school celebrity and success. In 1592 the list of minor candidates, sixty-four in all, records applicants from seventeen different counties of England. The provision in the 1560 Statutes that not more than one Scholar should be elected each year from the same county ensured a national rather than a local recognition of the School's advantages. Lord Burghley and his wife Mildred both supported the School with books and endowments, one with a perpetual annuity to be distributed to the Scholars elected to the universities, that by their training in virtue and learning 'they be made more able to serve in the Church of God and in the Common-wealth', the other by providing two exhibitions to St John's College, Cambridge. Deans of Westminster continued to take a close personal interest in the daily life of the School. Lancelot Andrewes (Dean 1601–5) used to take over the school work and correct the exercises for a week at a time, as well as teach Greek and Hebrew to older boys in the Deanery in an evening, and allow Scholars, one of whom was likely to have been George Herbert, to join him on his walks.

John Williams, Dean of Westminster and Bishop of Lincoln, added further scholarships to St. John's in 1624, as well as two fellowships reserved for Westminster students, though a subsequent note attached to these ordinances and statutes registering the inadequacy of the revenue tells a melodramatic story of Williams' intention, as he lay sick, of adding a further estate to increase the capital value of the benefaction. 'But it being somewhat late at night and his lordship much indisposed, he deferred the signing and sealing of them till the next morning, before which time it pleased God to take him out of the world.'

The distinction and the prosperity of Westminster in its early years are epitomised by William Camden, who was Second Master from 1575 to 1593, and then Head Master until 1598. As a young man of modest means, he had been befriended by Philip Sidney at Oxford, and raised to the fraternity of Renaissance culture. Through the mathematician John Dee he met Ortelius, the Flemish geographer and disciple of Erasmus, and became an assistant in Ortelius' project of making a map of the Roman Empire under the Antonine Emperors. So began a period of travels in Britain during school holidays, in search of the past. Chorography, as this empirical branch of history was known, had been stimulated by the threat of the sweeping away of evidence consequent upon the Reformation. Camden's researches led to the publication, in 1586, of his *Britannia*, written in Latin, which established him at once as a member of the European republic of letters. Camden's work for Ortelius had expanded, and he endeavoured to add Celtic, Saxon and Norman to the Roman eras of British history. His aim is declared in *Britannia*'s preface, 'to restore Britain to its antiquities, and its' antiquities to Britain'. Camden, encouraged by Burghley, became the historian of Elizabethan England. He founded the first chair of history at an English university and, in 1586, established the Society of Antiquaries with a group of friends which included Robert Cotton, a former pupil and collector of the manuscripts which are the glories of the British Library. Camden was much beloved by another celebrated pupil, Ben Jonson, who not only dedicated his first play, *Every Man In His Humour*, to his former teacher, but also wrote an affectionate and laudatory epigram linking Camden's personal qualities to his academic renown:

> Camden, most reverend head, to whom I owe
> All that I am in arts, all that I know,
> (How nothing's that) to whom my country owes
> The great renowne, and name wherewith she goes . . . .

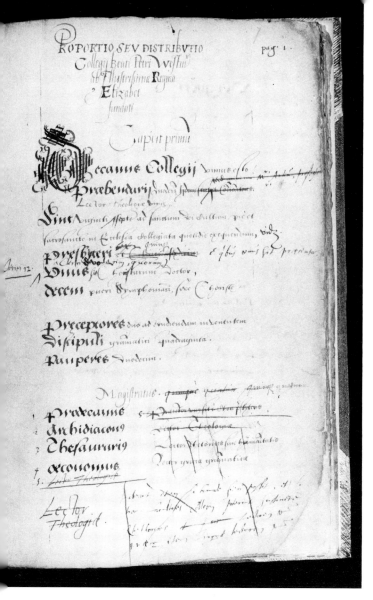

TO THE MOST
LEARNED, AND
MY HONOR'D
FRIEND,

Mr. Cambden, Clarentiavx.

SIR,

Here are, no doubt, a supercilious race in the world, who will esteeme all office, done you in this kind, an iniurie; so solemne a vice it is with them to vse the authoritie of their ignorance, to the crying downe of Poetry, or the Professors: But, my gratitude must not leaue to correct their error; since I am none of those, that can suffer the benefits confer'd vpon my youth, to perish with my age. It is a fraile memorie, that remembers but present things: And, had the fauour of the times so conspir'd with my disposition, as it could haue brought forth other, or better, you had had the same proportion, & number of the fruits, the first. Now, I pray you, to accept this, such, wherein neither the confession of my manners shall make you blush; nor of my studies, repent you to haue beene the instructer: And, for the profession of my thanke-fulnesse, I am sure, it will, with good men, find either praise, or excuse.

Your true louer,

BEN. IONSON.

A 2

The Statutes of 1560 (*left*). The first page lists the Dean, Prebendaries, Readers and Choristers, and then groups together 'Two teachers for the instruction of youth, forty grammar pupils, twelve paupers'. The School and Almshouse were linked, as in monastic days, as charitable institutions. Ben Jonson's dedication of his first play, *Every man In his Humour*, to his former schoolmaster, William Camden (*right*). From the 1616 Edition of Jonson's works in the School Library.

Camden, the only lay headmaster of the School until 1937, looked back on his time as a schoolmaster towards the end of his long life, in terms that catch exactly the spirit of the School's early years:

> I know not who may justly say I was ambitious who contented myself in Westminster School when I writ my *Britannia* . . . I never made suit to any man no not to his Majesty . . . neither (God be praised) I needed having gathered a contented sufficiency by my long labours in the School.

3

GLOVES FOR MR BUSBY:
1603–1695

T HE loss of Elizabeth's protection and care, at her death in 1603, ushered in a time of uncertainty. The School had to establish itself exclusively on its own merits in a period characterised by political instability, religious faction, and military conflict. That it survived the Civil War and the Commonwealth, and emerged at the Restoration in 1660 as the most distinguished school in England which produced an extraordinarily high proportion of the leading statesmen, politicians, divines, scholars, poets and philosophers, who embodied English civilisation in the next fifty years, was almost entirely due to the personal authority and academic distinction of Richard Busby, who was Head Master for fifty-seven years.

So favoured a first half century was perhaps too good to last; in its second half century the Tudor school became necessarily embroiled in Stuart political and religious turmoil in the eye of which it sat. An ominous note was sounded in the Chapter Minutes of 1608, which feared high prices and 'a great dearth of all things'. Two years later Richard Ireland was the first Head Master to find his position precarious. He joined the Catholic church and, presumably fearing exposure, fled to France. The ensuing 'bruit', touching Ireland's disposition in religion, led to a Chapter order that he was either to return from France or purge himself of the imputation. He did neither, and lost his job. Lambert Osbaldston,

Opposite. Dr Busby's monument in the South Ambulatory of the Abbey.

Opposite.

Queen Elizabeth I, who refounded the School in 1560 as part of the College of St Peter in Westminster (*top right*), which replaced the Benedictine monastery briefly reconstituted in 1556. She took a strong personal interest in the School's life, visited the early Latin Plays, and received volumes of verses dedicated to her by the Scholars. From a contemporary portrait in the School library.

Richard Busby, Head Master from 1638 to 1695 (*top far right*). 'The fathers govern the nation; the mothers govern the fathers; but the boys govern the mothers, and I govern the boys.'

Alexander Nowell, Head Master 1542–1553 (*bottom far right*). A distinguished scholar, who established the study of Anglo-Saxon in England, who made Terence the central figure in the curriculum. He was also well-known as a fisherman, and was the accidental inventor of bottled beer on one fishing expedition when he left some ale by the riverside in the sun. He survived into the next century, and was later Dean of St Pauls and of Windsor.

William Camden, Under Master 1575–1593, Head Master 1593–1598 (*bottom right*). Beloved by Ben Jonson, who dedicated his first play to Camden, and wrote a sonnet in gratitude to him Camden's famous *Britannia*, compiled during school holidays, was the first comprehensive survey of England's historical remains.

Head Master from 1622, and an eminent scholar, fared worse: he fell foul of Laud. We hear his panic in his petition to Laud of 1637, where he 'protests that he never had the least intent to wrong your Grace in any letter he wrote in his whole life', and 'prays to be preserved from public suits in law, which will ruin him'. Laud was unrelenting. The phrases 'little urchin' and 'the little meddling hocus-pocus' were too derogatory, and Star Chamber condemned Osbaldston to be dismissed from his mastership and his prebend, to pay a fine of £5000, and to have his ears nailed to the pillory in Dean's Yard in the presence of his Scholars. Fortunately he had wind of this indignity and disappeared in June 1638, leaving a trail of evidence pointing to France. In fact he appears to have taken refuge for three years in a garret in Drury Lane, emerging after the fall of Laud in 1641. He was to have his reward. In the Ordinance of the Lords and Commons relating to the College and Almshouses of Westminster of 1645 he is mentioned as the only Prebendary not to desert his charge, the rest being 'delinquents to the Parliament'. In the Act of 1649 for the Continuance and Maintenance of the School and Almshouses, he is allotted an annuity of £100 for the term of his natural life and continued to receive £25 a quarter until his death in 1659. Many Head Masters have shown a similar instinct for survival in adverse times.

Osbaldston's discomfiture in 1638 opened the door for Richard Busby, justly the most celebrated Head Master in Westminster's long history, and perhaps the most remarkable headmaster in the whole history of education. He succeeded Osbaldston in an acting capacity in 1638 or 1639, was granted patents by the Chapter on 23rd December 1640 at an annual salary of £20, and continued in that office for the next fifty-five years, spanning four reigns and the Commonwealth, dying in 1695, at the age of 89, still fearsome, in possession of all his faculties, and still Head Master. His personal capacity for survival, in physique and office alike, is no less remarkable than the shrewd power inherent in his preserving and enhancing the school and its fortunes in the troubled years of his tenure. The stability he embodied and the adaptability he displayed seemed to enter the very bloodstream of the place, so that at the desperate crises of its later history, in the 1840s and the 1940s, the Busbean instinct for survival somehow prevailed in defiance of all probability.

Westminster, and subsequent English culture, were fortunate in Busby. His tenacity to his educational and political principles, and his dexterity in avoiding potentially incriminating challenges to them, ensured that the School did not fall victim to the tides of faction that swept through or away other institutions. Indeed, his long rule seemed to imprint a pattern which resisted all tides for about two hundred years. When Liddell came to revise academic life in 1846, Ginger, the School bookseller, had to be compensated for his large stock of often reprinted Latin and Greek grammars, which Busby had introduced to replace Lily's Latin, and Camden's Greek, which were the standard text books when he took up his post.

The routines of School life, for generations, themselves become tide-like, subduing all who enter them to its inexorable force: the Latin Play at Christmas, the Challenge (the long-drawn out series of oral contests between minor candidates competing for scholarships) in spring, the Election and its accompany-

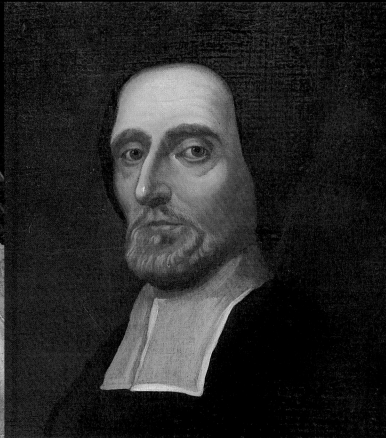

GVLIELM. CAMDEN   PRÆFECTVRÆ HISTORICÆ
CLARENTI.   FVNDATOR. MVNIFIC

PONDERE, NON NVMERO.

Hic oculos similes vultusq. hic ora tueri
Poteris, nec vltra haec artifex quiuit manus.
ANNALES ipsum celebrisq BRITANNIA monstrant
Perenniora saxo et aere muniuata.
Quisquis et Historicae Cathedrali hanc conscenderit esto
Benignitatis vsq monumentum Loquax

The monastic granary in Dean's Yard, which was the Scholars' Dormitory from 1540 until 1729. It was demolished in 1758, and its stones still support the terrace in front of Church House.

ing festivities in the summer, the distribution of Lord Burghley's bounty; the appointment of Dean Williams's Bishop's Boys (scholarships open to boys of Welsh descent marked by the wearing of purple gowns), the Scholars' bonfires on St Peter's Day, November 5th and Coronation Day; Scholars' feasts at All Hallows, Christmas, Twelfth Night, Candlemas (four legs of mutton in 1649), Shrove Tuesday, Good Friday, Easter, the Election, Whitsunday and St Peter's Day. The meal bills show that mutton was provided four times a week, and beef three times. What was left over from dinner was eaten cold for supper. There were pies for the Scholars every Friday and Saturday. The quantity of beer flowing from the College Brewhouse to the Scholars has a tidal quality about it too: 'A pottle a day a piece', or four pints per Scholar per day, one pint at dinner, one at supper, and two for beavers (at 8 a.m. and 3 p.m.); twenty-one gallons a day, 15 hogsheads every month, at a cost of 12 shillings per hogshead. And 'the beere is better than ordinary VIs beere. There is a quart^r of malt to every 3 hoggesheads'. The allowance of bread from the College Bakehouse is 64 loaves a day, for 40 Scholars and the Usher.

Each year the routines extend over 46 weeks, for the Scholars are reckoned to be absent only for the month of August, and for short vacations at Christmas, Easter

Opposite.

Little Dean's Yard in 1845 (*top left*), from the south-west corner: a colour version of the lithograph by Radclyffe. Notable features of this picture are the original porter's lodge to Ashburnham House, the boys playing racquets in the recess between School and College, and the Tudor 'pepper-pot' caps on the South Transept of the Abbey.

Little Dean's Yard in 1986 (*bottom left*). The old raquets court has disappeared, a new storey has been added to Ashburnham House, the Gothic pinnacles have reappeared on the Abbey.

33

and Whitsun. In some years, though, the threat of plague compelled long retreats to the rural delights of Chiswick, where the School was conducted for fourteen weeks in 1652, while in the Great Plague Year of 1665 Busby ordered the dispersion of the School for six months, though seemingly with a heavy heart. Each year, 149 yards of black cloth @ 9/6 per yard is ordered for the Scholars' gowns, and made up at a cost of 2/6 per gown. Every school day at Westminster from 1599 to 1883 the whole School gathered in the same room for its labours.

Even ostensibly momentous changes were at least as conservative as they were innovatory. In 1729 the near-derelict monastic granary in Dean's Yard was abandoned in favour of the new Dormitory adjoining College Garden built by Burlington. But the move substituted a classical building of almost identical proportions and layout, and housing an identical mode of life, for the medieval relic that had done improbable service since 1560. Apart from frequent hasty repairs to keep it standing, the only innovations there on record were the bringing in of a water supply in 1656, and the making of a 'pissing Cistern' in the chamber, for which a mason's bill of 1659 survives.

The relentless routines of the School must have driven the boys to seek palliatives, though there are few records of the unofficial side of Westminster life. One vigorous dormitory jest survives in a contemporary account.

> At Westminster School, the Monitor used to call the Schollars by 6 of the clocke in the Morning all winter long, and as soone as ever they hearde his Surgite they would skippe out of their bedds and away to prayers; Three or 4 Rakells observing two that were Beddfellowes to be very nimble and hasty upon their call, and their Bedd being placed under a great Beame; they contrived it so, as in the night in a dead Sleepe, they fasten cords to the Bedd and drew it up a great height; in the darke morning hearing the sumons of the monitor, out springs one of one side, and the other on the other side of the Bedd, and Bounc't against the floore, with a crackt crowne, soare Bones, and much hazard of their Neckes.

It must indeed have been a raw, rough existence at boy level. Mary, Countess of Caithness, writing in 1690 about Colin's experience as a new boy, catches exactly the apprehensions of boarding school mothers in all centuries:

> In the great cold Scoul he sitts the whole day over with out a hatt or cap; and all the windows broke and yet thanks be to God he taks very wel with it tho he never seeth a fir but in my hous; at the beginning his felow scolers wer hard on him upon the account of his Nation but he doth now hold up pretty wel ether at scolding or boxing with them; however I fear I los a Scotsman for he begins to get ther words and actsent . . . hear is a long story of nothing to you but he being my only companion maks me have littel other subject to writ of to you.

In July 1679, eleven Scholars were implicated in a murder. A woman brought a request for help from a neighbour in St Ann's Lane, of whose house and goods a bailiff was taking possession. The Scholars sallied out, motivated less by chivalrous zeal than by outrage at the infringement of ancient custom, the place being supposedly privileged against arrests. The bailiff was attacked, beaten with clubs, and subsequently died. Seven of the eleven fled; four were first committed to the Gatehouse prison, above the old archway to Dean's Yard, and then allowed extraordinary bail. All came to trial at the Old Bailey in October, but eight of them were granted a Royal pardon before proceedings were opened (the pardon still hangs on the wall of College), and the remaining three were acquitted. The law for the poor was unhappily more severe. Three other people, the woman who carried the news, another who invited them to go through her house, and a man who provoked them to mischief were all found guilty. It seems that Busby not only exercised his influence with the King, but may also have committed perjury to save his Scholars from punishment.

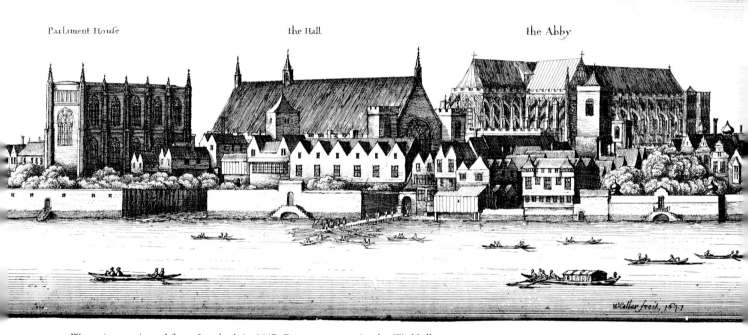

Westminster viewed from Lambeth in 1647. From an engraving by W. Hollar.

Only six months after Busby's appointment, the political situation in 1641, notably tension between the Long Parliament and Charles I, prompted the purchase of twenty muskets and 20lbs each of powder and musket shot for the College, and in the following year Westminster boys helped defend the Abbey against a mob of Puritans who 'would have pulled down the organs and some ornaments of the church' but for the stout resistance offered by Scholars, officers and their servants, who drove them out. A chain of such moments links the centuries. In 1386 Lytlington and two monks buckled on armour at the threat of invasion; in 1848, when Chartist rioters rampaged through the streets, Dean Buckland threatened to fell with a crowbar any of them who tried to enter the Abbey; in 1908, the Dean's Yard gates were closed for safety against the noisy crowds caught up in the Suffragette demonstrations; in 1916 James Gow signalled air-raid warnings by ringing a bell in Little Dean's Yard; in 1940 the Canons and Minor Canons, some still in frock coats, underwent arms and gas-mask drill in Little Dean's Yard.

From the ferment of religious and political debate of 1645 there emerged an Ordinance of the Lords and Commons which transferred the government of the College and Collegiate Church of Westminster from the Dean and Chapter to a committee of thirty-three, eleven lords and twenty-two commoners, with power to elect and choose Scholars. The committee ordered the holding of prayers in English morning and evening, and a good deal longer listening to morning sermons 'for edification in Catechistical lectures'. On discovering that each Scholar generally paid 10 shillings quarterly for their Commons, and 10 shillings more for tutorage, the committee esteemed it 'a dishonour to the Parliament that those poore boyes should be at that charge' and restored the free school, allotting Busby £50 a year as compensation. In April 1649 all Deans and Chapters were abolished, which prompted the Act for the Continuance and Maintenance of the School and Almshouses of Westminster in September of that year. Fifty-six governors were appointed, and all Abbey lands and rents were vested in them, to be applied to cover the total annual cost of just under £2000. It is curious that the eventual independence of the School under the 1868 Public Schools Act by parliamentary appropriation of ecclesiastical funds was anticipated over 200 years earlier. The blow to the Abbey's pride was perhaps greater in 1649 than in 1868 because the College of St Peter itself, as the Abbey Church had been formally known since 1540, was never formally dissolved despite the abolition of Deans and Chapters, so the School and Almshouses alone maintained the continuity of the Collegiate body for eleven years. Lists of St Peter's College compiled in 1649 and 1650 reflect the extent of the ruin: some are dead, some in prison, some in Oxford, some in arms at the parliament. Busby's name has an entry by it only once. He is 'sickly' in 1650 for the taking of the Covenant, the oath signifying acceptance of ecclesiastical reform. We must assume this to be shrewd strategy rather than cowardice, for we have Robert South's famous testimony to the Royalist character of Busby's, and his School's, sympathies: 'upon that very day, that black and eternally·infamous day of the King's murder, I myself heard, and am now a witness, that the King was publically prayed for in this School but an hour or two before his sacred head was cut off'.

The substitution of lay governors of Puritan sympathies for the largely Royalist Dean and Chapter seems to have wrought small change within the School. Complaints about the behaviour of the boys rather increase in proportion to the length of catechising and sermonising to which they were subjected; there is no diminution of the quantity of salmon, lobster, capons, geese, chickens and rabbits consumed at the Election Dinners of the 1650s. The appointment of a committee triggered a volley of petitions on behalf of potential Scholars, many referring to loss of estates in Ireland or to religious persecution as causes of distress. All magnify the merits of the sons and the poverty of the parents; never were so many young geniuses so much in want. Every device to jerk a tear and tug a heartstring is applied. One may stand for all:

Petition of Sarah, the Relict of Mr. John Vincent, sometime minister of Sedgefeild in the County of Durham, deceased. Sheweth That your petitioner's said husband being a most precious Godly Minister was persecuted by The Bps while they were in power, And since, during the late Warrs, was plundered of all his estate, And afterwards was put into a place 400 miles distant from that small estate which he left for the subsistance of your pet[r] and children, within 2 years after dyed, and left her a moste disconsolate Widdow, with seven most hopefull Orphans in a desolate farr Country and above 100[l] in debt. Yet your pet[r] hath made hard shift to bring up her 5 sonnes to Learning, the 2 youngest of them being now schollers in Westminster Schoole, and so are well-known to be very hopefull boys . . .

Busby himself was beset for a time by a contentious Under Master, Edward Bagshawe, who had apparently been appointed from Christ Church to foment trouble which could lead to Busby's removal, and his replacement by a candidate of the anti-episcopalian party, one Owen Price of Magdalen College. Through 1657 and 1658, Bagshawe told tales about the treatment of the boys, and grew outraged as his self-esteem was injured by Busby's continual outflanking. An observer describes him: 'He turns with a vengeance, goes over to the Gentiles, and that he might be revenged upon Mr Busby, sacrifices to Moloch, worships and adores the worse of men, even the Judges of King Charles I; but Mr Busby, who Plow'd with the same Heifers, had too much complyance, cunning, and money, to be hurt by him'. Busby was provoked at last to cut down the wooden staircase in the old dormitory, to prevent Bagshawe's access to his chamber. At this Bagshawe departed, to write his 'True and Perfect Narrative' of his differences with Busby by way of consolation. Some years later, after a contentious career as a churchman, he died, mad, in Tothill Street.

The ebbing of the Commonwealth and the flowing of Royalism was epitomised by an incident at Cromwell's funeral in 1658. Robert Uvedale, sixteen-year old Westminster Scholar, darted between the soldiery, snatched a silk banner, the Majesty Scutcheon, from the bier, and vanished into the crowd before he could be caught. The trophy now belongs to the School, after remaining for over 300 years with Uvedale's descendants.

It is an indication both of Busby's learning and his politics that, during the 1650s, the great aristocratic families start sending their sons to him. The Howards, Digbys, Newports, Ashburnhams, Wyndhams, Sackvilles, Russells and Montagues begin to vie, as a proportion of the School, with the sons of country gentlemen who had hitherto made up the majority of boarders. Busby's reputation as an educator was firmly established in his early years, and his learning was exceptional. His academic library, the core of which is still housed at the School in the room he had built by Robert Hooke, a pupil who had boarded with him in the early years of his headmastership, reveals him as a polymath. A collector of bibles in many languages, he also introduced the study of Arabic to Westminster, alongside the Hebrew which had been taught since the early seventeenth century. Ornithology, architecture, astronomy, mathematics, geography are all represented by the most advanced books. He had a copy of Descartes' *Discours de la Methode* very shortly after it was published anonymously at Leiden in 1637. A catalogue of his books, written in his own hand at the end of

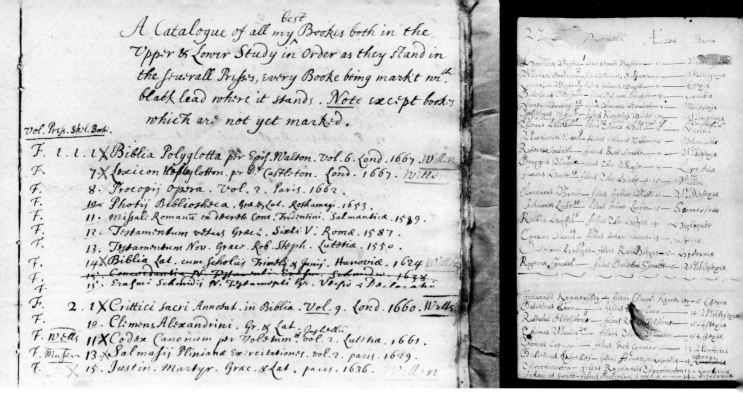

The opening page of Dr Busby's manuscript catalogue of his (best) books (*left*), compiled in the last year of his life, 1694, when he was 88 years old. The Challenge list of 1647 (*right*), showing the admission to College of John Locke aged 15 (14 entries from the top of the list), from Somerset, who only gained tenth place in the Election.

his life, conveys a caressing and painstaking pride in his collection. 'There were no indifferent people come out of his hands', wrote Steele after Busby's death, 'but his Scholars were the finest Gentlemen, or the greatest Pedants in the age. The soil which he manured always grew fertile, but it is not in the planter to make flowers of weeds. . . .'

John Locke came from Somerset to Westminster some time in the 1640s, and gained entry to College in 1647. His account book for 1649–51 begins with the purchase of 'an act for the School' (the parliamentary provision in the absence of Dean and Chapter), and records the acquisition of an impressive range of texts: Homer, a Greek grammar, Livy, Tully, minor poets, Godwin's *Greek, Roman and Jewish Antiquities*, a Hebrew psalter, Epictetus, Plautus, Lucan, Seneca, *Sententiae veterum poetarum*, Pliny, Virgil, Horace, Juvenal, Persius, and the works of Dr Taylor. There is homely detail too: 'pies against the election', 'foote out of snare', 'turnip seed for my mother', 'for the key of the schoole', 'for a paire of gloves for Mr Busby'. His recipe for 'Bugg Ale' reveals the prep school boy lurking in the philosopher, and begins 'Take six hundred sowes or woodlice, red sage and rue, of each a handful. Bruize them all together and put them into a canvas bag . . .' Such frivolity is entirely absent from his letter home just before the Election of 1652 in which he was elected to Christ Church. 'Most dear and ever loving father, my humble duty remembered unto you. I have to my utmost done what lies in me for the preparation both of myself and friends for the election . . . neither is Mr. Busby any way wanting, he having spoken to the Electors on my behalf, and although my Latin oration be not spoken yet he hath promised me that my Hebrew which I made since shall . . . Tuus obedientissimus filius John Locke'.

The career of the inappropriately named Arthur Godley was much less happy. A petition of 1656 to have him made a Bishop's Boy recommended him 'of more than an ordinary capacity to make a Scholar', but in 1657 we find him so unpopular that three monitors are compelled to lodge a written complaint against him.

He frequently curseth and sweareth.

He wished himself in hell that he might see his fellows there.

He asked for a knife to kill himself.

He went to drown himself.

He endeavoured to stabb himself, thrusting his knife through his doublet he cryed out murder when one of his fellows would have hindered him from stabbing himself.

He threatened to kill his fellows in their beds, bitt one of his fellow's arms, often beateth and abuseth them.

He ran away out, and would have run away twice before.

He often feigneth himself madd.

As to the dutys of the Colledge and his common manners he is irregular and disobedient in all things he allways speaketh english, wanteth exercise, is very slovingly and unclean in apparrell, maketh a noise everywhere. He observeth not orders neither submitteth himselfe to those that are set over him to give an account of his and others manners being a grievous example in the eyes of his fellows.

He disappears from the school list, and is never heard of again.

Humphry Prideaux arrived from Cornwall in 1660, with a letter from his uncle, hoping that his country rudiments will be no prejudice to his progress in learning. Under Busby's care they were no obstacle: he gained entry to College in 1665, became a Hebrew scholar but declined the Oxford Professorship of Hebrew, wrote a Life of Mahomet and died Dean of Norwich. Lists of minor candidates of the early 1660s suggest that there must have been many such 'country rudiments' arriving hopefully at Westminster in search of advancement: 14 counties furnish 25 candidates in 1660, 21 counties furnish 30 in 1661, with all parts of the British Isles represented.

Busby's educational regime was thorough and severe. A minimum of seven hours a day was spent in the Schoolroom, with an inexorable sequence of tasks linked with each period of the day, each day of the week. Aesop on Mondays, Ovid on Tuesday, Terence on Wednesdays, Martial on Thursdays, for those in the Second Form. Construing first, dictionary work second, then translating, then parsing. After dinner dictation in English, to be made into Latin. On Fridays repetition of all the week's exercises, a habit which persisted until the 1850s. There are many continuities in both the form and content of the curriculum which persist for over 300 years, consolidated by tradition and by the scale of Busby's achievement.

For the Elizabethan curriculum, closely modelled on Eton's, survived with only minor modifications until the middle of the nineteenth century. Terence and Aesop dominate the early years, Ovid the middle years, Homer and Virgil the later years in school. The writing of verse begins in the Third Form, the study of

John Dryden's name carved on a pine bench Up School. It was destroyed by incendiary bombs in 1941.

Greek in the Fourth, when the Bible, Psalter or Liturgy in Greek began to be studied in place of the Latin Testament and Cathechism. Martial was often in the Westminster curriculum as a master of epigram, Justin the Martyr for his edifying example. Anthems and works are chosen for their propriety and their elevation of sentiment or style. There is no Tacitus, no love poetry, no Greek comedy, little evidence of interest in history. In the emphasis given to the study of Greek, to facility in verse and to acquaintance with Hebrew, Westminster's curriculum was unique. Add to the narrow range of writers native to this curriculum the most frequent though to modern tastes surprising visitors, Dionysius and Isocrates, and the mixture of pride and regret that characterises Gibbon's appraisal of his Westminster days (1749–52) becomes intelligible. 'I left school with a stock of erudition which might have puzzled a doctor, and a degree of ignorance of which any schoolboy would have been ashamed'. Such schools 'may assume the merit of teaching all that they pretend to teach, the Latin and Greek languages: they deposit in the hands of a disciple the help of two valuable chests'. But for every disciple who found the treasure there must have been scores who had no capacity for the search. An anonymous writer in the *Gentleman's Magazine* of 1739 is content to celebrate the gradations of the School as a decorative and immutable sequence, natural, beyond question, like the order of the stars:

'Ranged into seven, distinct the classes lie,
Which with the Pleiades in lustre vie.
Next to the door the First and least appears,
Design'd for seeds of youth, and tender years;
The Second next your willing notice claims,
Her members more extensive, more her aims;
Thence a step nearer to Parnassus' height,
Look 'cross the School, the Third employs your sight.
There Martial sings, there Justin's works appear,
And banish'd Ovid finds protection there.
From Ovid's tales transferr'd, the Fourth pursues
Books more sublimely penn'd, more noble views.
Here Virgil shines; here youth is taught to speak
In different accents of the hoarser Greek.
Fifth—these more skill'd and deeper read in Greek,
From various books can various beauties seek.
The Sixth in every learned classic skill'd,
With nobler thoughts and brighter notions fill'd,
From day to day, with learned youth supplies
And honours both the Universities.

It is small wonder that Busby's school became an early tourist attraction. John Evelyn, visiting in 1661, was more readily impressed than Swift in 1711: 'I heard and saw such exercises at the Election of Scholars at Westminster School to be sent to the University, in Latin, Greek, Hebrew, and Arabic, in themes and extemporary verses as wonderfully astonished me in such youths, with such

Opposite. Busby's Westminster. The rod-table and rod-drawer, at which Head Masters from Busby to Scott presided over the Schoolroom. A birch rod with the business end outwards, as in the picture, signalled the end of term; on normal school days the rod was reversed. The two Restoration chairs have prominent carved crowns; that on the right is supposed to have been given to Busby by Charles II. The selection of Busby's books on the table include a large Mercator atlas of 1638, the year of Busby's arrival at Westminster. (*Inset*) The surface of the rod table on which dozens of eighteenth and nineteenth century boys have left their mark.

readiness and witt, some of them not above 12 or 13 years of age'. But, feeling that he has been too easily impressed, he is impelled to offer two reservations, one worldly, the other pedantic: 'Pity it is that what they attain here so ripely they either not retain or do not improve more considerably when they come to be men, tho' many of them do; and no lesse is to be blamed their odd pronouncing of Latine, that out of England none were able to understand or endure it'.

Busby's discipline no less than his instruction was a by-word for severity. He called his rod his sieve, and declared that whoever did not pass through it was no boy for him. A favoured pupil, Philip Henry, later a nonconformist minister, records in 1647 that he 'felt the weight of Busby's hand' and deserved it, though afterwards 'he gave me sixpence and received me again into his favour'. Lady Dolben wrote of her sons being 'under the lash of Westminster School' in 1676. Sneer, in Shadwell's *Virtuoso*, declared that he came to the brothel to be flogged because 'I was so us'd to't at Westminster School, I cou'd never leave it off since'.

As late as 1785, Busby's reputation as a flogger was still so strong that a popular political cartoon above the title 'Dr Busby settling accounts with Master Billy and his playmates' commented on William Pitt and his taxation policy. Another eighteenth century image of him, Pope's portrait in *The Dunciad*, links the castigation of body and repression of mind in a nightmarish portrait with no redeeming feature.

> When lo! a Spectre rose, whose index-hand
> Held forth the virtue of the dreadful wand;
> His beaver'd brow a birchen garland wears,
> Dropping with Infant's blood, and Mother's tears.
> O'er ev'ry vein a shudd'ring horror runs;
> Eton and Winton shake thro' all their Sons.
> All Flesh is humbled, Westminster's bold race
> Shrink, and confess the genius of the place:
> The pale Boy-Senator yet tingling stands,
> And holds his breeches close with both his hands.
> Then thus. 'Since Man from beast by Words is known,
> Words are Man's province, Words we teach alone.
> When Reason doubtful, like the Samian letter,
> Points him two ways, the narrower is the better.
> Plac'd at the door of Learning, youth to guide,
> We never suffer it to stand too wide.
> To ask, to guess, to know, as they commence,
> As Fancy opens the quick springs of Sense,
> We ply the Memory, we load the brain,
> Bind rebel Wit, and double chain on chain;
> Confine the thought, to exercise the breath;
> And keep them in the pale of Words till death.
> Whate'er the talents, or howe'er design'd,
> We hang one jingling padlock on the mind.

The theatricality of this spectre's appearance and language was undoubtedly true to Busby's character, as to that of many another lesser schoolmaster. He had won high praise from Charles I in 1636 for his performance in Cartwright's *The Royal Slave*, and had apparently contemplated a career as an actor. Though there is no evidence of regular plays at Westminster in Busby's time, we have Barton Booth's assertion that he took part in a Senecan tragedy in 1693, and played the lead in Terence's *Andria* in 1695. When Booth ran away from school in 1698, aged 17, to join a group of strolling players in Dublin, he carried with him no less of Busby's influence than the bishops, poets, scholars, lawyers and men of science who were his more orthodox pupils.

There is a ferrety meanness about Busby's expression recorded in portraits and busts, and undoubtedly his interest in money was sharp. He was criticized for taking into his own house far more boarders than he could look after (over thirty at one stage), and his surviving account book, though muddled, records every detail of fees, personal expenditure and the biannual gifts, usually of money, which his pupils were expected to provide. His correspondents in Wells, where he was appointed Prebend and Treasurer of the Cathedral in 1660, are full of anxiety and apology when writing to him on financial matters. The dilatory library keeper who had failed to carry out improvements that Busby had demanded was relieved at the news of his death which reached Wells in 1685. When the news turned out to be false, his obsequious letter of excuse is abundant evidence of the terror he could inspire in adults as well as boys. 'Devilish covetousness' was the phrase Pepys used about him after a conversation with Lord Ashburnham, Cofferer to Charles II, who had become a near neighbour in 1665 when he took up residence in Ashburnham House. Humphrey Prideaux writes to John Ellis in 1677 about their former Head Master: 'Old Busby hath long talked of a benefaction he intends to bestow upon us (in Oxford) for the erecting of a catechist lecture in the University, but hath so many cautions in his head and adjoynes such hard conditions with it that the University cannot receive it'. He then records another of Busby's indispositions, which may have been tactical, as at the time of the Signing of the Covenant. 'The old man a little before Christmas spit blood, and thought he should have immediately dyed, but when I was with him I thought him as well as ever I saw him since I knew him.' The yearly expectation of his death for the last twenty years of his life further increased the wonder he aroused.

His tight-fistedness put him in a position to show much generosity to those in need. It is clear from his accounts that many Scholars unable to pay any fees received a free education at Busby's hands, often ten or more a year. There are many testimonies to the kindness with which he treated suppliants in distress, and did his utmost to make provision for their sons, if they showed promise.

From the Restoration onwards, he was invulnerable. In 1660 he was appointed Prebend and Treasurer at Westminster as well as at Wells, and from 1672 he was Archdeacon at Westminster. His Scholars, during their time at school as well as in after life, were prominent in the life of the city. At the Great Fire of London the Dean, John Dolben, collected the boys together and marched with them on foot 'to put a stop, if possible, to the conflagration'. This quixotic gesture was rewarded by their success in saving St Dunstans in the East from the conflagra-

An extract from Dr Busby's Account Book, 1656.

tion. Thomas Taswell, who was one of their number, records that on the next night, when the fire blazed up again, 'went to royal bridge in the New Palace at Westminster to take a fuller view of the fire. . . . About eight o'clock it broke out on the top of St Paul's Church, already scorched up by the violent heat of the air and lightening too, and before nine blazed so conspicuous as to enable me to read clearly a 16mo edition of Terence which I carried in my pocket'.

Busby's confidence was great. He kept his hat on his head when Charles II visited the School, on the grounds that his pupils 'must not think there is a greater man in the land than myself'. The King approved this notion, and presented Busby with a Head Master's chair which is almost a throne. George V also liked the story when he paid a visit to the Pancake Greaze in 1919, and commanded James Gow to remain covered. Westminster Scholars made their first recorded appearance at a Coronation in 1685 for the coronation of James II, a precedent which has been followed at every subsequent crowning. The self delight in one of Busby's favourite observations is justified by the School's celebrity: 'The fathers govern the nation; the mothers govern the fathers; but the boys govern the mothers, and I govern the boys'.

He was able to brush aside an anonymous and savage letter of complaint about the neglect into which the School had fallen in 1690, when he completed 50 years as Head Master. The author ends by threatening him that the souls of all whom his want of discipline has ruined will appear as witnesses against him 'at the Dreadfull day (which considering his age cannot be long)'. But the dreadful day was still five years ahead. Busby died on 5th April 1695, at the age of 89, with an entirely appropriate theatrical accompaniment. People in the street, when he was expiring, saw 'flashes and sparks of fire come out of his window, which made them run into the house to put it out, but when they were there saw none, nor did they of the house'.

Robert Creighton, son of Robert and father of Robert, had written to Busby in 1686 when the third generation of the family entered into Busby's care. His gratitude and affection shine from his letter, which should stand as a just and final tribute to Busby's extraordinary achievement.

'The school I send him to will make him happy or nothing will . . . Good sir, help my cares, and after all your cares of me, when my youth was under your direction and government, let me, instead of requiting you for all those cares, beg you to add to your cares one more. Those doors of the best school in the world which once were open to grandfather and father I know you will not shut against this child. You see, Sir, your cares are never at an end, your labours are immortal: children come and beg to be under the same care and protection their fathers were, as if they claimed the privilege of giving trouble to Westminster School by prescription. Thus I run into a new debt before the old be satisfied . . . to you I owe my education, and my childs, my fortune, my fellowship in Cambridge, my Lecture there, my travails, my Station in this church, this Dividend, myself, all, except my infirmities.'

4

POLITE YOUNG RUFFIANS:
1695–1803

EIGHTEENTH century Westminster was Busby's triumph. He had won the battle for public schools over private tutors, and the golden age of the School predictably followed. It grew and flourished on a scale that would have astonished the pious foundress. By 1727 there were over four-hundred boys in the School, and reliable report suggests there were, at one time, five hundred, numbers not equalled until the 1950s, and not exceeded until the 1970s. The events the School generated were subjects of both cultured and popular interest. Eighteenth century newspapers abound in School news, gossip and sensation; the aristocracy patronise the School in large numbers, and five future Prime Ministers are educated there; Old Westminster dinners and the annual Latin Play in the new Scholars' Dormitory become reference points in the calendar of the life of fashionable London; the boys behave in a style and with a confidence that breeds more admiration than censure. Dramatist Richard Cumberland, a boy at school in the 1740s, sums it up in his memoirs: 'There is in that School a kind of taste and character, peculiar to itself, and handed down perhaps from times long past, which seems to mark it out for a distinction, that it may indisputably claim, that of having been above all others the most favoured Cradle of the Muses'.

It is not surprising that the Dean and Chapter, discovering their fledgling turning rapidly into a cuckoo, should largely ignore it, making occasional efforts

A lithograph of 1845 by C. W. Radclyffe which shows Burlington's Dormitory as it was from 1729 until 1847, when the open arcade was enclosed and turned into day rooms for the Scholars.

to repress its burgeoning dimensions. The Chapter minutes are preoccupied with the division of the spoils from great services, the income from the sale of sites for slabs or tombs, fabric funds and repairs, the improvement of the locality, fines imposed upon absent prebendaries. Only twice are they stirred up by school affairs: both occasions involve the expansion of the School, and both lead to litigation.

The first was the building of a new dormitory for the Scholars, to replace the ruinous granary. Under the forceful championship of Dean Atterbury, a new site was chosen in the College Common Orchard or Garden, which the now elderly Christopher Wren, Surveyor of the Fabric, was induced to approve. George I, the Prince of Wales, and Parliament were petitioned, and between them contributed well over half the total cost. A series of Baroque designs by William Dickinson was rejected in favour of a new Palladian design by Burlington, freshly returned from a tour of Palladio's Italian buildings which he had made in 1719. There was much alarm and dissension in the Chapter, however, complicated by the absence of many of the pluralist prebendaries for long stretches of time. Dr Dent took the lead: 'We neither do, nor can give consent to a thing so prejudicial to our rights and detrimental to the good of College'. But the headstrong Atterbury would

The terrace at the southern end of Dean's Yard, just before its demolition. It was built in 1760 as part of William Markham's clearance of the yard and his attempt to establish boarding houses in the precinct. The stone platform, which still remains, was built from the materials of the Granary which the Scholars used as their dormitory until 1729. The second house from the right was where Busby's was first established as a boarding house in 1926.

have his way: the foundation stone was laid in 1722 and the Dormitory occupied in 1729, though with blind windows facing into the Chapter's closely preserved garden secrets. Ironically Atterbury did not see the completion of his scheme. Charged with high treason on account of his Jacobite sympathies, he was imprisoned in the Tower and exiled to Brussels before much more than the foundation stone was in place.

The Chapter was fluttered again in 1755 when Head Master William Markham brought in a bill for clearing away the alleys and tumbledown buildings, relics of the monastic farm, at the south end of Dean's Yard, and building a terrace to bring boarders, scattered among enterprising landladies in the vicinity, into the Abbey precincts. The canons declared that life would be insufferable and the neighbourhood terrorized, but the terrace was built. Life turned out to be not so insufferable, since landladies and parents seemed disposed to prefer the old system, and Markham's dream was not fulfilled. It seems that the paths of the Abbey and the School had begun to diverge 150 years before their legal separation: the Dean and Chapter recognised no responsibilities to any pupils but the 40 Scholars on the foundation, and regarded the running of the School as a business venture on the part of the Head Master and Ushers. The longest-running squabble in London, about the name and use of College Garden, began its still unfinished two hundred and fifty year history early in the eighteenth century. 'College' in this title refers, of course, to the whole collegiate body, and not, as many have supposed, to the residence of the Scholars. The attempt to rename it the Abbey Garden has exacerbated feelings without resolving confusion.

Despite the School's growth in numbers, buildings, and favour, the force of continuity is massive. Between 1695 and 1803, eleven men are Head Masters and Under Masters. All eleven were former King's Scholars, six were from Christ Church and five from Trinity. Five served as Under Master before their appointment as Head Master. Thomas Knipe spent 53 years at the School, Pierson Lloyd 52, William Vincent 46 and John Nicoll 44. The eleven average over thirty years of service. Each year the Election festivities consume 'sparrow-grass', anchovies, capers and olives, salmon, flounders, eels, soles, saltfish, lobsters, lumpfish, geese, chicken, pigeons, duckling in lavish quantities. Each year cloth is bought at 8/- a yard, 3½ yards per scholar, and is made into gowns for 2/6 a gown. Most years the Chapter Minutes make a despairing gesture towards boy containment. 'Many idle boys' are disorderly in the Cloisters, and a beadle has to be appointed; they climb over the wall into College Orchard, so the wall has to be raised; they break the School, Library and College windows, so Dr Knipe is ordered to admonish them; they go up into the Belfry and cut the lock on the door to the Tower; a window is boarded up to prevent the boys getting in Dr Taylor's house, and a large fence put up to keep them from Dr Blair's Brewhouse.

A plan of the precinct of 1711, clearly showing the extent to which both Dean's Yard and Little Dean's Yard were built up.

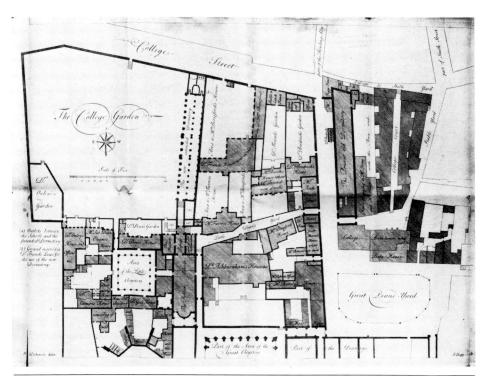

Opposite.

School in about 1840 (*top right*). A watercolour by G. R. Sargent.

College Dormitory in about 1840 (*bottom right*): an oil painting by G. R. Sargent. This barn of a building, with its three fireplaces reserved for Senior scholars, the public character of its everyday life, and the array of domestic duties which Juniors had to perform, has been subdivided after its destruction in 1941 into three floors, with over thirty rooms, including a rifle range.

Around 1740 four Scholars carve their names on the Coronation Chair to celebrate their sleeping there overnight, presumably on different occasions; in 1766 another reaches into a broken tomb and steals the jawbone of Richard II, returned by the boy's family a hundred and forty years later. The windows in the Old Dormitory had been boarded up because no glass stayed intact; in the New Dormitory too the windows were kept broken in deference to tradition.

An engraving by R. Pollard from a painting by R. M. Page, showing Scholars playing marbles in the Cloisters c. 1800.

The School was both a magnet and a mirror for the fashionable world, and held pre-eminence over Eton until well into the century. The *London Chronicle* in 1760 saw the politics of the previous thirty-five years as a conflict between the products of Eton and Westminster:

> As, on a board well poised, boys sink and rise
> As scales one falling, t'other upward flies.
> The sons of Westminster and Eton School
> Hold, in affairs of state, divided rule.

In 1750, parliament has a predominance of Westminster members, but by 1790 the balance had shifted in favour of Eton. In 1788 a Westminster magazine called *The Trifler* was founded as a rival to Eton's *Microcosm*, and bristled with both envy and satire of the court patronage enjoyed by Eton under George III's court at Windsor. Westminster began the eighteenth century with Tory, or even Jacobite

Burlington's Arch (*left*), intended as a gateway to both College and the Schoolroom. It was constructed in 1734; this watercolour, by A. G. Vickers, depicts the arch in 1831.

sympathies. The 1715 Rebellion in support of the claims to the throne of the descendants of James II commanded the loyalty of Dean Atterbury and many Westminster boys. One at least, Lord Erskine, was unafraid to give a spirited reply to General Stanhope in 1716. He was the nine-year-old son of the Sixth Earl of Mar, attainted earlier in the year. 'Pray', said the General, 'mind your book and learn not to be a rebel like your father'. The young Lord put his hands to his sides and with a stern countenance told him that 'that matter was not yet decided who were the rebels'.

The young Prince William of Cumberland visited the Latin Play in the New Dormitory on at least two occasions in the early 1730s, though the Prince of Wales had already noted the School's disaffection. The adoption of a new motto 'In Patriam Populumque', which first appeared in the 1750s, marked the Whig sentiments which were to dominate for the remainder of the century. Political sympathies had done a volte face in the thirty years since the 1715 Rebellion and Lord Higham Ferrers, later Marquis of Rockingham and Prime Minister, even ran away from school to fight the Jacobites during the new Rebellion of 1745. A lover of escapades, he had dressed as a fashionable young lady a year or so earlier

The Latin Play c. 1890, set against a backcloth designed by C. R. Cockerell in 1857.

and induced John Nicoll, the Head Master, to show him around the School. Nicoll was aghast shortly afterwards to see his visitor being well doused by boys under the pump in Dean's Yard.

Nicoll's genial mildness, his liberalism, his encouragement of a code of honour among the boys seemed ideally suited to an independent minded school strongly supported by the aristocracy. A 1733 manuscript list of noblemen educated at the School contains sixty-two names in one generation. Zachary Pearce, Old Westminster and Dean, preaching the Bicentennial Sermon in 1760, is in no doubt that the School is in its Golden Age: 'Thus planted by Queen Elizabeth, and duly watered, and skilfully cultivated, the School, from being at first like the grain of mustard seed, has since grown to be a mighty tree, under which a great part of English nobility have had their education'. The patronage of the great families, however, did not divert Head Masters from Busby's tradition of academic achievement as the criterion of esteem. When a nobleman's son asked Markham to point out to him the place appointed for boys of his rank, the Head Master directed him to the lowest seat on the lowest form. Men who valued a place in society above humble scholarship did as John Hinchliffe, son of a livery stable keeper, who resigned the Head Mastership in 1764 after three months in order to be tutor to the Duke of Devonshire, a position from which he rapidly rose to be Master of Trinity and Bishop of Peterborough simultaneously. But his fickleness was exceptional, and most preferred to devote their lives to what *The Public Advertiser* in 1755 called 'the first Seminary of School Learning in Europe'.

However admirable or thorough the learning, it is the vigour and range of the boys' lives out of school that strike the modern observer as exceptional. At one moment they are invoked by the leading intelligences of the day as paradigms of precocity; at another they are engaging in violent and lawless diversions in which their youth and social class alone, as in the episode of the Bailiff's murder in the previous century, save them from the rigour of the law.

Their reputation for virtuosity was established in the seventeenth century through their public performances at the Election, and in the eighteenth it was consolidated by the Latin Play which, from being an occasional event in Busby's time, came to share with the Election both pride of place in the School's year and its public celebrity. A comedy by Terence or, occasionally, by Plautus was re-established as a Christmas festivity, echoing the medieval practice, soon after 1700. The performance was the prerogative of the Scholars, and took place in their own chamber, first the Granary, then from 1729 the New Dormitory. The moving of many of the beds to set up a stage and seating was a disruption of domestic routine, which persisted with the unquestionable certainty of seasonal change until 1938, the School's last Christmas in London before the destruction of the Dormitory in 1941. Even during the collapse of the School's fortunes and reputation in the nineteenth century, the Latin Play remained one of the principal events of London's winter season, which royalty, foreign ambassadors, leading politicians, archbishops and bishops, as well as distinguished Old Westminsters used, as a matter of course, to attend. It was a kind of academic Derby Day, reported in full by the major newspapers, and occasionally cancelled as a mark of respect in a year of the death of a member of the Royal Family. In 1858, Prince

51

Albert attended, and took with him the future Edward VII. Victoria records in her diary: 'Dear Papa is still not quite well – he went yesterday evening with Bertie (who understood not a word of it) to see the West[r] boys act one of their (very improper) Latin plays'. Originally, no doubt, shared Latinity could be taken for granted, though there must have been many nineteenth and twentieth century visitors who were largely bemused by play, place, performers and the event as a whole, and by the distinction, if any, between English tradition and English eccentricity. The distinction would have been entirely lost on the small Town Boys who were co-erced into occupying 'The Gods', a high and narrow plank at the rear of the auditorium. They held on throughout the performance by one hand, but when directed by the 'Mon. Gods' had to clap with two, or else be caned on legs and thighs. To add to their ordeal, they were made to run the gauntlet of the Junior Scholars on their way in and out of College, and normally ended bruised black and blue for their pains.

Alexander Nowell, in the 1540s, had first introduced Terence to Westminster, and the clear and expressive speaking of Latin was then an important attribute of statecraft. In the sixteenth century, performance of plays was both a practical and

A sketch of 1873 showing the scale of the construction that took place each year in College Dormitory to set up a stage and eighteenth century style theatre, with a separate pit for the ladies.

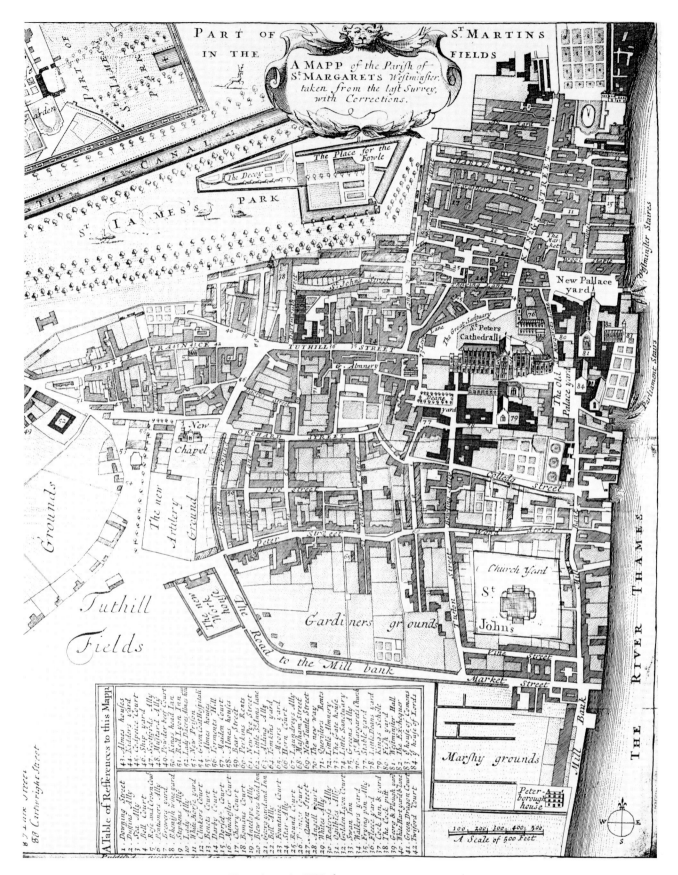

Westminster in 1755: from a contemporary map.

a diversionary exercise of that attribute. The purely dramatic pleasures of Terence have seldom been eulogised. Nonetheless, like a fly in amber, performances became preserved for over two hundred years with audiences steadily decreasing in comprehension long after the original justification for the plays had disappeared. From 1704 onwards, embellishments and compensations were annually offered in the form of Prologue and Epilogue. The Prologue was generally written by the Head Master as an elegant, metrically exemplary, review of the year, including achievements and deaths of notable Westminsters. The Epilogue, generally written by an Old Westminster, consisted of satirical comment upon topical events, spoken by the cast, their Terentian or Plautine identities transferred to the present, and based upon verbal puns, and the games playable when current events are presented in a Roman perspective. In the first surviving Epilogue, to the *Amphitryon* of 1704, Louis XIV and the War of the Spanish Succession are the subjects; in 1783 Montgolfier and his balloon; in 1789 the Fall of the Bastille; and in 1812 Napoleon is caricatured by the braggart Gnatho in Terence's *Eunuchus*.

The Latin Play was the main artery of a diversified theatrical passion that possessed the School for most of the century. Performances spilled over into the West End. Otway's *Orphan* was presented at Hickford's Dancing Rooms in Panton Street in 1720; *Julius Caesar* in the theatre by the Opera House in 1728. After the first night of *Beggar's Opera* in 1728, Swift wrote to Gay: 'Lord, how the school boys at Westminster, and University lads adore you at this juncture'. Pope, discussing posthumous fame with Lord Mansfield, declared that the surest method of securing it would be to leave a sum of money to be laid out in an entertainment to be given once every year to the First Form of Westminster School for ever. The testator would by this means ensure 'eulogisms and Latin verses to the end of the world'.

The idea and the fact of 'performance', in plays, in the great Schoolroom, in valedictory orations, in epigrams on given themes before the College, in the challenge up to 1855, in end of term Orations up to the 1970s, reinforced from without by the proximity of great public events, of Parliament and, until 1834, by the law courts, and by the popularity of London theatres and pantomimes, accounts entirely naturally for the theatrical character of the School's everyday life, its sense of style, and the professional preferences of its pupils, as marked today as at any other point in its history.

Eighteenth century journalism abounds in reports of the initiatives taken by Westminster boys to enforce their own law over anyone else's, including the law of the land. Acts of lawless insouciance include the rescue of a schoolfellow who had uttered false money from the Gatehouse Prison or Madam Hughes from an officer who had arrested her for debt. In the Dean's Yard affray of 1779, eleven boys assault a man in Dean's Yard and with knives drawn threaten to rip him up. The magistrates were inclined to be severe: but the sentence of a month in Bridewell and a fine of £100 stood only for an hour. When a father told them that his son would forfeit his election to Christ Church unless he went there in a few days, the Court took off his imprisonment, and then voted to release the others from theirs. The £100 was reduced to £50, which their friends paid, and all were

The reverse side of Burlington's archway of 1734. Burlington intended this entrance as the gateway to both the Schoolroom and to College Dormitory, which he had completed in 1729. From 1779 onwards, boys paid Abbey stonemasons to carve their names on the arch, on the interior walls of School, and in the Dormitory.

released. For such conduct in our time, the School and the adults in it would bear a large measure of censure. It is hard for us to realise how axiomatic it was then that the authority of Head Master and Ushers extended no further than the Schoolroom, and even there it was often tormented to a degree which modern teachers and their unions would scarcely credit. One boy became adept at firing paper darts smeared with cheese into the 'plaguily severe' William Vincent's wig, in order to hear him call out in his nasal voice 'I smell cheese'; the Duke of Richmond set fire to Vincent Bourne's greasy hair in order to be able to box his ears on the pretext of putting out the flames. The size of the School, the attractions of the town, the background and affluence of many of the pupils, and the diversity of their living arrangements made unified control as difficult then as now. As the School flourished, enterprising landlords and landladies moved into the area and advertised boarding houses for young gentlemen, which were, of course, wholly independent of the School and resisted Markham's attempt to institutionalise them in the 1750s. It was only towards the end of the century that Ushers began to be attached to these boarding houses to provide an official, if often ineffective presence. Grants, the school's oldest boarding house, takes its name from a family who ran a private establishment from the 1750s; until as recently as 1935 the same house, though belonging entirely to the School, was still run primarily as a private business venture, with the Housemaster standing the risks involved. Edward Gibbon's aunt, Mrs Porten, ran another boarding house in Great College Street from 1748 to 1762 before moving to Markham's terrace in Dean's Yard. The advertisements for boarding houses placed in the newspapers vie with one another in their claims to defend health and morals, to provide elegant accomplishments of gentility such as French and dancing, and to amplify the School's narrow curriculum with 'other necessary branches of learning, exclusive of those taught at the School: writing, accompts, geography, several useful branches of the Mathematics'. This lucrative trade was much favoured by Huguenots and by clerics; an average charge would be £20 per annum for boarding, with five or six guineas more for schooling.

With domestic life, out of school activity, and a large part of a boy's education, out of the School's control, it is not surprising that there was much lawlessness within the precincts too. The Abbey Cloisters were the favourite arena for many violent contests, without regard to the safety of the inhabitants, the solemnity of the services or respect for tombs or architecture. In 1716 the publisher Edmund Curll was rash enough to stray into Dean's Yard after pirating an oration spoken by John Barber, Captain of the School, at the funeral of Robert South. He was seized, tossed in a blanket, and then thrashed to the great glee of Pope who celebrated the episode in *The Dunciad*. The only evidence we have of adult intervention is defensive. In 1760, when five hundred poor inhabitants of Westminster, brewers, servants, gardeners, assembled to revenge the many insults they imagined to have received from the Westminster Scholars, the Masters, learning the intentions of the mob, locked the Scholars up.

The inflammation of political feelings by the revolutions in America and France towards the end of the century may have disposed pupils to dramatic conflicts with authority, for which authority sometimes found dramatic solutions. A rebellion in School in 1786 was quelled only by the Head Master, Samuel Smith, taking a thick stick and knocking down Francis Burdett, one of the ringleaders, and so presumably launching him on his tireless career as radical and reformer. Another fracas five years later was at first thought to have destroyed Dr Vincent's authority for ever, and was attributed to 'French democratical principles and the doctrine of the rights of man, which had crept into the School, and had been rankling for some time'. *The Public Advertiser* offered an earthier account, suggesting that the cause of the conflict was simply the boys' refusal to return to School from watching a fight. The episode ended humiliatingly with the flagellation of the Captain. Vincent chose to take issue with an anonymous magazine which appeared in 1792 called *The Flagellant*, which made outspoken comment on Vincent's disciplinary methods. A character called Mr Thwackum claims the divine right of schoolmaster, but the author counters it with the assertion that 'all that have fallen under my knowledge are illiterate, savage, and unrelenting'. Then a letter from 'Thwackee' sets out to prove that flogging was invented by the Devil, and that 'whosoever floggeth performeth the will of the devil'. The Head Master, outraged, took out a libel action against the publisher, as a result of which the three editors, one of whom was Robert Southey, future Poet Laureate, had to confess, and were expelled.

The enterprise, the taste for adventure and the independence of mind and action grounded in their schooldays may account for the important parts played by Westminsters in North America, in India, and in support of the French Revolution, as well as the surprising number of prominent dissenters to emerge from so emphatically Anglican a school. Arthur Middleton signed the Declaration of Independence in 1776, and in 1777 W. H. Drayton was elected President of South Carolina. Charles Pinckney was A.D.C. to Washington, and his brother Thomas U.S. Minister to England in 1792. Warren Hastings was only one of many Westminsters who went East as administrators or justices: thirteen combined to present an elephant-handled silver cup in 1783, which still stands on the Scholars' table in College Hall each day of term. Westminster news was a regular feature of the *Calcutta Gazette* in the latter part of the century.

Among regular diversions for youthful energies and aggressiveness, cricket was enjoyed at Westminster at least as early as at any other place in England. Lord Chesterfield, in a letter to Philip Stanhope in 1745, in wishing that he played cricket as well as any boy at Westminster, implies that it was well established though rivalled by the older game of pitch-farthing. The Sackville family provided several players, and Lord George was a participant in the first cricket match of which details are preserved, in 1746, between Old Westminsters and Old Etonians. A first Scholars v. Town Boys fixture is recorded in the 1780s; there may have been a match with Eton in 1786, and there was certainly one in 1796 at Hounslow Heath, despite the hostility of the Eton authorities. William Lamb, the future Lord Melbourne, opened the batting for Eton.

We should not be deceived, though, by this early evidence of the channelling of schoolboy vigour into competitive sport, into thinking that we are approaching modern times. The more characteristic leisure activities were individualistic, and involved degrees of risk and tolerance we find quite alien. Tuttle Fields, or Tothill Fields, the vast area of low-lying meadow and swamp now covered by Pimlico and Belgravia, was a playground of rich potential. The site of the great Tothill Fair in the Middle Ages, it came to serve a double purpose, of recreation for citizens ('bowles, goffe and stoolball' in the seventeenth century) and, roamed by pigs, 'the receptacle of half the filth of the metropolis', the stench of which did not deter the younger George Colman from keeping there a phaeton and a pair of donkeys, called Smut and Macaroni. Because the Fields belonged to and were administered by the Dean and Chapter, Westminster boys had acquired the status of privileged users, and even had a skating pond specially dug for them. Here fox and hounds games, beagling, and snipe-shooting were engaged in, the headquarters being a former pest-house called Five Chimneys, where guns, liquor, tobacco and women were to be had. Sam Husbands fell into 'the embraces of a vile, wicked strumpet' in 1755, and contracted 'the foul disease', but Markham was ready to have him back in School on his recovery 'because he was a lad of parts'. Two years later, though, in one of those topsy-turvy judgements that remind us

Twenty-two Old Westminsters, headed by Warren Hastings and Elijah Impey, sent a silver cup from India in 1787 to show affection for their school. It still stands on the high table in College Hall for formal meals.

The Five Chimneys, Tothill Fields. A favourite place of resort for Westminster boys in the eighteenth and early nineteenth centuries, especially for the hire of guns for shooting snipe, and of skates for winter sports.

of our historical distance, he was expelled for lying in bed too late in the mornings. Rats provided a major interest. They ate their way through the wainscoting in School, and ran about during lessons; at night they took possession of the Dormitory, running over the beds and dragging off food and clothing. Boys devised miniature cannon to fire at them, and rented a row of ruinous houses on Millbank where they broke through the interior walls in order to hunt them more freely. The river, unembanked, provided still more excitement. Roberts, a boatman between Lambeth and Vauxhall, would provide boats for the young gentlemen. They may not have been very safe, for there are memorials in the North Transept and East Cloister to Archibald Hamilton and Albany Charles Wallis who drowned in 1744 and 1776 respectively. You were only a little more fortunate to be pulled out of the river and restored to consciousness by Roberts, whose remedy was to apply the blade of an oar smartly to the most sensitive part of a young gentleman's anatomy.

There is little mention of the ill-treatment of boys by other boys in the eighteenth century; perhaps the concept of bullying is anachronistic, and such hardship was too normal for comment; perhaps Nicoll's code of honour held until manliness became a conscious ideal. There was fagging, to some degree, though Colman's comment 'blacking shoes and running on errands are rather redundant parts of a liberal education' is mild in comparison with the criticisms that were to develop in the first half of the next century. Surviving letters of younger boys reveal, once the initial terrors of the place have been endured, a rather matter-of-fact robustness and resilience:

Freddy Reynolds, aged 11, wrote home in misery on his second day at the School:

> My dear dear Mother
> If you don't let me come home, I die – I am all over ink, and my fine clothes have been spoilt – I have been tost in a blanket, and seen a ghost. I remain, my dear dear Mother,
> Your dutiful and most unhappy son, Freddy.
> P.S. Remember me to my father.

Thomas Fawcett, in 1779, also aged 11, has gathered his wits about him, but is still proud of his little successes and appalled at the conduct of his school fellows:

> Dear Papa, I can do verses a great deal better than I used to do. I make all my own verses now without anybody helping me. I have taken a great deal of pains since you left London last and I hope to comfort you in everything that is in my power. The boy that thieved so many things was fetched to school today . . . Doctor Smith flacked him but not near enough he deserved twice as much for such a boy as he is ought not to be let do such things it will be the ruin of him for ever. He is hated by all the school and not be spake to by any of the boys.

Whereas Henry Mills, in 1783, aged 14, is much more the worldly young gentleman:

> My dear Mother, I must own I have been very negligent in writing, but you must not suppose it entirely out of Idleness, for I have had a great deal to do both in the writing and fagging for the Seniors, but you may now give me Joy of being a Second Election Boy. I intend being very studious this year to make up for my last . . . I intend having a pair of Buff Breeches and laying by my silk ones till the Winter again . . . Dickins got in second into College. He will have a sweating year of it. – The hardest watch I ever had was last Tuesdays the last night I did not get off till between Twelve and One, I had not a small number of lickings in that Time.

Boswell's anxious fussiness about his son's entry and early experiences at Westminster in 1790 were probably uncharacteristic of parents in general:

> I awaked in great concern about my son James, who I feared might be ruined at Westminster School. I had today a letter from Veronica, . . . mentioning that little

James plagued her for money and that she was afraid Westminster was very expensive. In his handwriting was subjoined this paragraph: 'Pray, Sir, is not Veronica to give me some money as, if I am at Westminster, I must not be a miser?' This little characteristical trait revived me immediately, after having been so sad about him. But I could not help being apprehensive of danger to his morals.

The priggishness hinted at in Fawcett's letter is much more obtrusive in the school career of Augustus Toplady (1752–3), later hymn writer ('Rock of Ages, Cleft for me'). He spent a whole holiday in 1753 preaching a sermon to his aunt (who gave him a shilling) on a text from Isaiah. His regular prayer on going into school ran:

O Lord God dear Redeemer, heavenly Father, dear Protector, grant I may not have any anger from Dr. Nicoll, Dr. Lloyd or any of the Ushers, they may proceed from any one cause whatever, and in particular (here I name my fears) . . . Amen. Grant also I may not have any Quarels with my Schoolfellows. Grant that peace may circulate in our hearts as if we were brothers. Amen.

Perhaps his righteous incongruity led directly to an entry in his journal for March 10th: 'Had a vast bad hard slap from my Usher, for all I carried him gold but the Thursday before'. A hard and painful lesson for an earnest boy in a hard school, and a timely reminder that fun in retrospect was often only the consolation of memory for a norm of anguish and fear which was and is the staple of many school lives. The glow which follows William Cowper's sending his imagination on a thirty year journey, back to his boyhood in the 1740s, perhaps reflects more the human compulsion to reconcile ourselves with our past than to recall it accurately. But let it stand as the epitaph to 'the Golden Age'. He fancied himself:

once more a schoolboy, a period of life in which, if I had never tasted true happiness, I was at least equally unacquainted with its contrary . . . accordingly I was a schoolboy in high favour with the master, received a silver groat for my exercise, and had the pleasure of seeing it sent from form to form for the admiration of all who were able to understand it.

5

READY TO FIGHT EVERYBODY:
1803–1919

V ERY different from Cowper's benign imaginings were the expectations of
Cyril Jackson, Old Westminster and Dean of Christchurch. Writing to Henry
Wickham, a Junior in College in 1803, he was in no doubt that the boy's
experience would be, indeed ought to be, purgatorial as well as comradely:

> Let me see you whenever I first meet you as a King's Scholar, such as a good junior
> ought to be, somewhat miserable, tolerably dirty, very obedient, trying always to
> laugh rather than cry, decently mischievous, despising cakes and oranges, and aware
> that money is of value to a King's Scholar only as it enables him to buy good cold
> meat, and that a bit of cold beef and a draught of porter, eaten and drunk by stealth,
> perhaps in the dark, and shared with another Junior, who possibly had no money
> that day himself, is the sweetest morsel you will ever eat.

The new century, and William Vincent's promotion from the headmastership to the Deanery, mark the beginning of a great change in the School's
fortunes. Mismanagement, or non-management, by four successive Head
Masters, neglect by the Dean and Chapter, the rapid transformation of London,
the foetid deterioration of the Westminster neighbourhood, and a boy-run society
which institutionalised servitude frequently accompanied by brutality set Westminster on an inexorable course of decline which reduced its numbers from 332 in

1818 to a paltry 67 only twenty-three years later in 1841, and almost brought its history to an inglorious end. The rest of the period covered by this chapter is characterised by the hard labour of regaining a lost reputation, which brought premature age and death to the three Head Masters concerned, Scott, Rutherford and Gow, after their Sisyphean toil. The labours of Scott and Rutherford were additionally burdened by protracted and acrimonious public disputes, one with the Dean and Chapter in the wake of the Public Schools Commission, the other with Old Westminsters and masters angry with Rutherford's attempts at reform. The history of Westminster in the nineteenth century is unique. Untouched by the Arnoldian spirit, it remained a time-encapsulated decadent eighteenth century institution for much of the century, self-regarding and largely isolated from other schools.

After the shift of royal favour to Eton under George III, the only member of the royal family to notice Westminster was the grand old Duke of York, who urged all his military friends to send their sons there as preparation for roughing it in the army. William Carey, Head Master 1803–15, chose to make fighting the School's leading feature. 'When I was a boy at Westminster', recalled Augustus Short, later Bishop of Adelaide, 'the boys fought one another, they fought the masters, the masters fought them, they fought outsiders; in fact we were ready to fight everybody'.

It was an earlier Westminster generation who provided Wellington with many of his best officers, and of whom he was reported to have said that 'when he entrusted any order to a Westminster, he was sure it would be carried out'. Carey's boys, and very many of their successors, took up military careers; the conduct of Raglan and Lucan in the Crimean War does not reflect well on either the School where their habit of mind was formed, or the army which it supplied.

Fighting at Westminster took many forms. Baron de Ros kept fighting cocks under the floor of his dormitory; bull and bear baiting were common entertainments at 'The Five Chimneys'. Sparring matches in houses were organised by heads of house, and up to 1875 there were frequent 'mills' in the Milling Green at 7 a.m.: open-ended bouts of single combat on the Green in the middle of the cloisters, more usually reduced to a mud-patch by the feet of combatants and the ring of spectators that always formed about them. Tom Vincent's first fight, in 1830, was with a bully two years older. After nearly an hour's spillage of blood, both fighters were reduced to exhaustion. Vinegar and water was applied for twenty minutes before they went to School. Vincent's anxious mother, relating the episode in a letter, hopes that good will come out of evil. But the pretexts were not always so laudable. Robert Bruce Dickson was challenged in 1861 because he got out at cricket before his partner, the last man, had received a ball. Larger scale warfare was practised in Dean's Yard, which was felt to be territory to be defended against all comers. The all comers, largely coal-heavers, draymen, butcher-boys and carriers, likewise felt that their right to cross the yard was to be asserted at all times. The 'scis' or 'skies' (no consistent spelling exists), as they were known (supposedly from the Volsci), were challenged when they dared to set foot on the Green, or when they refused to throw back a ball that had been kicked off during a game. General skirmishes seemed to be the preferred form of exercise,

Caxton's House in the Almonry in 1826 (*above left*). The Almonry stood to the west of the Abbey, and the densely packed streets of this part of Westminster were swept away by the construction of Victoria Street in 1851.

Little Sanctuary in 1807 (*above right*), from an engraving by J. T. Smith. The Sanctuary stood to the north of St Margaret's Church, near the foot of the present Whitehall, so Smith appears to have taken the liberty of moving the west towers of the Abbey into his view.

The stairs to School (*right*): eighteenth century stone; nineteenth century inscriptions.

with the skies generally coming off worst, and being simultaneously revived and humiliated by being soaked under the Dean's Yard pump. The running dry of this pump in 1865, allegedly caused by the construction of the Metropolitan Railway, dealt this sport a more or less final blow. The relationship between boys and skies was obviously a variant of the Town and Gown rivalry in the older universities, but seemed to contain elements of mutual, if begrudging respect, which gave it a symbiotic character. Though the inhabitants of the foul tenements and alleys to the south were denounced as 'blackguards' or 'the great unwashed', they would enthusiastically line the railings of Vincent Square to cheer on Westminster teams until after the First World War and bestow nicknames on the players: 'Darkie', 'Rice 'orse', 'the Convict'. If ever they dared venture inside, however, they were set upon: the rich man in his playing field, the poor man at his railings. While the School was populous, Westminster boys had little trouble physically, and still less morally, in getting the best of the skies. Some Scholars were reproached with cruelty when they injured a local boy in 1829. Their self-justification was: 'We are not to blame at all. It is no fault of ours that we use stones in this way, for Dr Goodenough won't allow us sticks'. The lines of battle, so clearly drawn when two sides are involved, are more fluid when there are three. In 1858 there was 'a snowballing row with blackguards at the entrance to Dean's Yard. Some of the masters came to stop it, and got their hats knocked off.' G. A. Henty's account, in *Captain Bayley's Heir*, of a street battle with skies during his Westminster days (1847–52) is well known; fresher, and breathlessly fearful, is R. G. Challis' letter home in 1837:

> All I wonder is how people can possibly live in Westminster . . . sometimes a party of fellows go round and ring all the bells and knock at all the doors then sometimes they smash windows at othertimes they pelt everybody they see with horse chestnuts they used to have fights with the skies (i.e. blackguards) but now there are so few fellows the skies lick us it is really dangerous to go far from Dean's Yard in one direction without there are several of you. I went once with three or four fellows and the skies collected into a band of about a dozen or two and commenced the attack by throwing dead cats at us.

Sometimes the local affray would merge with wider political unrest. Clarence Paget and friends, in the 1820s, taking their cue from the masters, took to the streets crying 'Down with Burdett the Radical!' during a parliamentary campaign, but the mob laid hold of them and gave them a rough time. In 1830 mobs rioted on the street every night, fighting the new police; there were fights in the School over the Reform questions, and, during the Chartist Riots of 1848, the bigger Westminster boys were made special constables.

The liberties enjoyed by Westminster boys in the first half of the century owe as much to adult indifference as to their own uncivilised impulses. The Abbey was a playground they could swarm over unchecked, up the towers, along the triforium, round the outside ledges, and there were many days off school for such freedoms to be indulged in. Saints Days ('Red Letter days') were whole holidays; in addition Head Masters chose to declare 'early plays', which gave boys their liberty, on comparatively slight pretexts or even on a whim, once the hour of

Opposite.

Little Dean's Yard (*top right*): an early nineteenth century oil painting.

Dean's Yard in 1815 (*bottom right*): a watercolour by William Capon. Much of the east side of the Yard is still recognisable; to the right of the view, though, is the Scholars' Coffee House, on the site of the monastic Brewhouse, which projected into the present area of grass.

school before breakfast was completed. When the surprise announcement took place, the whole school rose and ran down School in joy as at the end of a term. The energetic could use such a day by taking an eight down river to Greenwich and back before dinner, and up river to Richmond and back before 'lock hours'. The less energetic were cast upon the town, or rampaged destructively in boarding houses not fully under the School's control. The curriculum contained only Latin, Greek and religious exercises; there was no French, writing, or arithmetic, except poorly taught as extras by hacks on half holidays; there was no usable library. 'The masters knew the customs of the place, and did not expect well-prepared lessons', reported William Smythe, who was sent by boat from Perthshire in 1816 for his Westminster education. The unfortunate Edward Jekyll failed to meet even the lowest standard, however, when he was admitted in 1815, aged eleven. Asked to conjugate 'amo', he launched into 'amo, ames, amet', and was immediately flogged and placed at the bottom of the School. An honest exchange between J. S. Bull and J. B. Campbell in 1818 about their teaching responsibilities finds comfort in the money to be made (up to £800 with a few private pupils) from 'quick botching', and in the prospect of passing vacations at the houses of parents. It is no wonder that there was small respect even for Head Masters. When Edmund Goodenough announced in 1828 that fags were no longer to perform menial duties, the older boys conspired to 'book' him: to throw all their books at his head Up School, a favourite and common expression of disapproval, with the supposedly liberated fags laid on to supply the ammunition. Goodenough stopped and harangued them from the middle of the room, and overawed them by his presence. Richard Williamson, his successor, much disdained because, though an Old Westminster, he had been only a Town Boy, had to use the displeasure of Christ Church and Trinity electors as a threat to stop a rowing match with Eton in 1834. He was denounced in the sporting journals of the city, and in the School Water ledger he is memorably vilified as 'that never to be mentioned, sneaky, spy-retaining, treacherous, cowardly, snivelling, ungentlemanlike, treble damnable shit of a Head Master of Westminster School (merely an M.A.)'.

Between 1833 and 1835, the School's population was halved, from 210 to 108. Old Westminsters who had in the past loyally supported the School began to send their sons elsewhere. It was suggested, and not only by the husbands, that mothers were beginning to have a larger say in their sons' education, and were aghast at the tales they heard from Westminster. A parent and an Old Westminster, Allen Cooper, wrote to Williamson in 1841 about his son's first year in College: 'You will grant, I am sure, that a parent has some little ground of complaint when he sees the face of his son disfigured, or his hand mutilated, or it may be his legs lamed, and that no notice of the circumstance has been taken by the Master or the Dame . . .'. A figure such as Jane Austen's Robert Ferrars thirty or more years earlier might have deserved Cobbett's famous strictures about the milksops attended by nursery maids who became the 'frivolous idiots' turned out from Winchester or Westminster; in the context of the 1830s the sneer is ludicrously inapposite: it was not a namby-pamby or affected place, but a wild and brutal one. At the lowest point of the School's history, in 1841, a Dirge of

College Hall (*top far left*): a view showing the Elizabethan additions, the gallery at the south end of the hall, and the refectory tables in the foreground.

College Hall (*top left*): the view from the gallery towards the High Table, backed by the coats of arms of Westminster, Christ Church, Oxford, and Trinity College, Cambridge.

Ashburnham House (*bottom far left*): the grand staircase, probably designed by William Samwell in 1662.

A metropolitan school (*bottom left*): the press of rooflines, architectural styles and building materials crowd the view north-westwards from the roof of Ashburnham House. The Abbey Song School rides high to the left of the Cloisters; beyond them are the Deanery, the early nineteenth century Gothic Sanctuary Buildings, and in the background the dome of Central Hall.

Westminster laments 'the guardianship of aliens and the natural neglect of step-parents'. In 1846 urgent representations were made to the Prime Minister about the state of the School, and particular Williamson's morally dubious relationship with Goodenough, the Captain of the School, and a Commission set about an enquiry. It appears that some whitewashing took place in exchange for Williamson's resignation; his letter to the Dean and Chapter is full of querulous self-pity and implicit acknowledgement of guilt: the late Commission is 'a wrong and an injury, tho' the results not discreditable. I have been hardly dealt with, and my credit and my authority must have been lessened in the world and in the School'. He departed for his parish at Sutton Coldfield and, in an unthinkable violation of tradition, Henry George Liddell was appointed to succeed him, the first Head Master since Camden in 1593 not to have qualified through a Westminster education to preside over the School's mysteries.

Fortunately, he had support in his stable-cleansing. Samuel Wilberforce, Dean briefly in 1845, had recorded that 'the School is in a dreadful state and very much, I feel sure from the need of greater comforts, cleanliness, and attendance, which we ought to supply. If you treat boys as savages they will be savages'. His stay at the Deanery was too short for him to act on his words, but his successor, William Buckland, was full of reforming zeal and the trio of Liddell, Buckland and Lord John Russell (O.W.), assisted by Palmerston, set about renovation and replanning. Liddell tackled the curriculum, and discarded Busby's Grammars; Buckland appealed for funds for College, and provided a sanatorium, breakfast for Scholars (for which they had previously to attach themselves to other houses), dayrooms by enclosing Burlington's open colonnade, and improved food in College Hall. Food inflames the passions of boys perennially. Earlier in the century demonstrations against bad food were called brosiers, and took the curious form of the consumption of every morsel of the offensive stuff, a kind of masochistic eat-in. Not surprisingly one boy died during one in Goodenough's time. Reform, especially of food, is not always appreciated by schoolboys, and on the day when treacle puddings were introduced, the College cook was summoned to have them hurled at his head. The intractability of the place was embodied in the drains. In 1849 Buckland dug up the precinct in order to replace the medieval drainage, and the cholera epidemic that followed caused a disbanding of the School. It is not surprising that Liddell quickly arrived at the view that there was no future for Westminster in its existing form and on its traditional site. 'Even if an angel from heaven were to come down, I do not believe the School's fortunes could be retrieved as long as it remains in London'.

Escape from the city was a theme which was to occupy Westminster periodically for the next hundred years, and it took the enforced stay in the country between 1939 and 1945 to convince everyone that its proper place was in the town. The rural rides in search of a new site made in 1850 by Liddell and Russell, occasionally with Prince Albert, fortunately proved fruitless.

More intractable than treacle puddings or drains, and less susceptible to influence, was the structure of boy society. Not until the hearings of the Public Schools Commission in 1861 and 1862 expose some of its worst abuses do the adults even begin to acknowledge it as a problem. One of the chief features of this

'College John' in about 1885.

Nineteenth century Westminster: a silk scarf and pink cricket blazer, a Monitor's tanning pole, cut with notches for each victim, quills and a glass dip which Juniors had to carry, filled with ink, in their top pockets, and an edition of Terence's *Adelphi* with a contemporary graffito.

society, indeed, was its self-regulating, adult-proof character. 'The Second Master never came in without warning, and if he had, he would certainly have been kicked out', recalled William Smythe of his College years (1816–22); in Pennyman Worsley's diary for 1858, Weare, his House Master, is mentioned twice, and the second contact arises only because Worsley has concussion and there is anxiety about his condition. Within College, a social system arose that was, in Smythe's phrase, 'the finest oligarchy that could be conceived'.

A complete system of duties and obligations linked older and younger boys in a network of feudal ties. For his first two weeks in the School, each new boy (the Substance) would be assigned a second year boy (his Shadow) to initiate him into his new society. During that time, the Junior was exempt from all punishment, and if he erred, his Shadow would be punished in his place. Thereafter he would be a dogsbody accountable to all Senior boys, as well as being linked with one as a personal fag and appearing on a rota of specific services to the House. The dignity of the Senior was further enhanced by his possesion of a Second Election (second year) boy as a personal vassal, who generally slept in the Senior's cubicle, and attended to his clothes and possessions and received the benefit of his patronage. The neatness of the system was that the Second Election boys were the slave drivers who ensured prompt compliance of the Juniors with their masters' demands, and who risked punishment themselves for a Junior's failures. The theory and, undoubtedly, often the practice was that obedience was matched by protection: for instance, when Juniors went out to local shops to fill tuck baskets, and brought back food to cook for their Seniors on the College fires, a portion of food was always reserved for the fags. Doubtless there were benefits in such a system: the instilling of loyalty and a sense of comradeship, even of life-long friendship, the merging of group identities; but it is easy to see how intolerable this system could be for conscientious, delicate or sensitive boys. If a Senior wished to rise early to work, the Junior called 'Light-the-Fire' would have to be up half an hour earlier, often at 3.30 or 4.00, to light a fire, boil a kettle, and

67

call the Senior every half an hour until he chose to rise. It was a disingenuous argument advanced to a Commissioner's enquiry about the impossibility of Juniors ever attending to their own academic work, that such early rising gave them an ideal opportunity for it. All day in College or anywhere in the precincts, each Junior had to respond promptly to the call 'Election' shouted by any Senior; he had to provide Seniors with pens, paper, ink, and penknives at his own expense; in School he had to move about at a loping run, touch the Monitors' table and place paper and quill in its drawer each time he passed it, and obtain leave from a master, a monitor, and his own Senior in order to leave the room for any purpose. Rather than have clocks put up in three rooms in College, Seniors preferred to call 'Clock', to which the nearest Junior had to respond by giving the precise time in a precise form of words (to say 'five and twenty' which compelled the Senior to do an addition was a punishable offence); rather than the Chapter's hiring a servant, one Junior each day was on 'Watch' duty, staying out of School and guarding the entrance to College. Many tasks – cleaning shoes, candlesticks, pans, tables, and carrying in wood – would have been performed elsewhere by servants; the parsimony of the Dean and Chapter unfortunately became reinforced by ritual. In the evening, before lock hours, 'Watch' had to call 'Will you please to take anything by orders? John is going off', and might be licked for getting a word wrong. This call meant that the door of the College was about to be locked, and that a servant, always called 'College John', who was stationed outside the locked door until 10.00 p.m., was about to go on errands. The Juniors had to organise the orders and the finances for 'John' to do a round of the neighbourhood shops, and his purchases would be pushed into College through a hatch on his return. It seems that nothing was prohibited: wine, rum and 'shrub' – a mixture of rum, sugar, and fruit juice – were favourite orders. Locking the boys in was the blind eye of the masters; from 5.45 in winter, 6.30 in summer and, most extraordinarily, in the afternoons of half-holidays, boys were locked into College with no adult present. The range of punishments for neglect of duties included the application of racquets, the edges of College caps, penknives or canes to various parts of the anatomy, 'buckhorsing', in which the unfortunate's head was used as a punch-bag, or 'tanning in way', when he was made to stand in the washroom, one leg raised on a sink, while a Senior took a running kick at him.

As grim as the incessant slavery to Seniors or to the whole house, and as the seemingly inescapable punishments from Seniors or from Second Election boys, was the ossification of the system into elaborate and sacrosanct customs and mysteries, many details of which are chronicled in ledgers, and, the clearest signs of institutional narcissism, the growth of an incomprehensible argot to defend them. As late as 1880, College was a jealously guarded secret society, which no Town Boy was ever allowed to enter, in which meticulous attention was paid to the manner rather than the substance of daily routine. The standard punishment for the merest inaccuracy was four strokes of the cane while you touched your toes, and yet curiously this was not felt to be a disgrace, but rather a glorious endorsement of the system. At the end of a year, the Junior who had received most punishments of this kind was congratulated.

There were two other formalised relations between older and younger boys. One was the Challenge, an oral examination for admission to College protracted over many weeks between February and May. In the presence of the Head Master as judge, the 'Minor Candidates' challenged each other on translation and grammatical rules based on the set texts, Ovid and the Greek Epigrams, so that each day their rank order changed according to the dexterity of question and answer. The candidates employed 'helps', boys already in College, who took on the task of preparing the challengers for their long ordeal, in return for a reward of about £15 when the exam was complete. These helps were present, rather like counsel, to argue niceties of interpretation before the Head Master, and to seek his favourable arbitration for their own candidate. This system, of 'mutual examination by the boys themselves', as the new regulations of 1870 worded it, obviously reinforced the conservatism of the place, and the ending of the exclusively oral Challenge in 1855 was a necessary release from suffocating tradition. On the final day of the Challenge, successful minor candidates, as if to prepare them for the ordeals ahead, were tossed high in the air from a blanket in the Schoolroom, to the refrain of a Martial hexameter: '*Ibis ab excusso missus ad astra sago*' and the 'Liberty Boy', who finished at the head of the list, was formally released from the duties of a Junior with the phrase '*Liber esto, ceteri servi*', and then 'chaired' round the precinct on a ladder carried on the shoulders of the scholars in a disorderly frenzy of celebration.

Grants House before 1868, gathering around the steps with an informality which within ten years had given way to a much more regimented style of group photograph.

The second ritual was 'Declams', or Declamations. At the end of the Juniors' year, they were required to write doggerel verses upon the Seniors they had served in the preceding months, and recite them before the rest of the Scholars. Though the event was a rowdy ordeal, performed by candlelight on the top of a pyramid of furniture, with the audience trying to put out the candle with missiles, it was accepted that the Junior had complete liberty to express his views of his Senior, and the Senior was bound to accept them without reprisal. Here at least was some guarantee of a curb on a Senior's conduct.

Before the Public Schools Commission of the 1860s, the only serious questioning of the system of fagging had occurred in the 1820s and 30s, when the emancipation of slaves made the issue topical. Minor concessions had been made by Goodenough and Williamson: Juniors were no longer to make the rods with which they were themselves beaten, but servants were to be employed instead. Town Boy fags were released from shoe and candlestick cleaning but, as the *Morning Post* ironically commented, 'such an inversion of the first principles of nature had never been heard of, and an embryo rebellion was the consequence'. When the Head Master was hissed by all, including the small boys, who had been ordered to do so the *Post* draw parallels with the plight of 'Jamaica juniors'. One enlightened scholar, R. J. F. Thomas, left College in 1827, giving as his reasons, in a letter to Lord Colchester, the arbitrary tyranny in the hierarchy, the helplessness of appeal to adults, and his apprehension that, having been tyrannised over as a Junior, he in turn would be a tyrant and 'despise the dictates of humanity'. Part of the system's power, naturally, was this self-perpetuating tendency. George O'Brien, a Senior summoned before the Commission in 1862, made the point exactly: 'In none of the fagging have the fags any interest, except that it does them good, and they look forward to the time at which they shall have similar advantages themselves'. A few minutes later he was involved in this bland and laconic exchange:

Q. What is considered bullying at Westminster?
A. There was a fellow put in a cupboard and smoked.
Q. What had the unfortunate boy done?
A. Nothing I think. That was the reason why it was considered bullying.

'Suts', the school tuck shop on the corner of Great College Street and Tufton Street shortly before its closure in 1903.

Giving evidence before the same Commission, 'Bunk' Ingram, Under Master (1861–80) approved of fagging. It taught a boy to be 'manly and independent'. Feeling that a more balanced view was needed, he added that to have a fag was pleasant, but not altogether good, while to be a fag was good, but not altogether pleasant. Seven years of frustration, however, are latent in Charles Broderick Scott's weary answer to the question 'Do you think the fagging system a useful one?' 'I do not see how to alter it.'

When not in School and not locked up, Westminster boys lived a self-sufficient life. Many trades-people had moved near to the precinct to provide a wide range of goods for them. In Great College Street, Sutcliffe's, a tuck shop which stood until 1903, was favoured for coffee, sugar, gingerbread, herrings, sausages and hardware. Further along was Ginger's, the school bookseller, Martin's, the school cobbler, and Vickers, a lending library. In Barton Street, Shotton's provided confectionery and beefsteaks, and sent mutton, hares and other game ready dressed into the houses. Oysters and fruit were to be had at Wise's, but if you were up early you could 'skip up town', hiding your hat en route, for a preliminary breakfast of oysters in Hungerford Market, now Charing Cross Station, before Early School. An old man called Baldwin appeared daily in Little Dean's Yard to sell racquets and balls to boys playing on the open-air courts in corners of the yard. Another regular visitor would give epileptic fits for a shilling at a time. Up on the roofs were many hidden corners for smoking, and for watching the fires that were always breaking out in the locality. On the Green in Dean's Yard mass football games occurred, the entire width of the green at each end, thirty yards or so, being designated the goal, and defended by about twenty 'muffs' or weaklings who were considered too feeble for the rough and tumble of play, which included handling the ball as well as kicking it. Despite the growth of London, the Thames remained fit to bathe in off Millbank until the mid-1840s. At low tide the boys were able to walk across the river above Westminster Bridge, and the water was so clear they could see their toes all the way. When a Mr Crunden was found guilty of bathing in the sea at Brighton in 1809, shocking sensibilities by undressing and dressing on the beach, the defence counsel argued

according to the principle contended for by the prosecution, all bathing in the Thames must be put a stop to, and that Millbank, at which the Westminster boys have from time immemorial been accustomed to bathe, is fully as much exposed to public view as the East Cliff at Brighton.

In 1825 Goodenough put up canvas screens, and the sport continued. Boating remained largely a private pleasure: most boys who wished were on the water most days in a variety of craft, engaging in the favourite pursuits of bargee baiting, leaping aboard a barge and pelting the operator with his own coals, and 'humbugging', charging broadside on the penny steamers which the populace had begun to patronise.

The shop keepers and skies had their fun at the boys' expense, however, each St David's Day. After a member of the old-established Westminster family of Williams-Wynn had visited the School for Latin Prayers, presented a guinea to each boy who could claim Welsh descent, and asked for a holiday, the whole

The Fields in 1845, looking north-east, showing the encroachment of new buildings and the necessity of a fence to protect the rights of Westminsters secured by William Vincent in 1810.

school set off for Battersea for the annual ditch-leaping across the marshes of what is now Battersea Park, the older arena of Tothill Fields having largely disappeared under Pimlico. The ditches all had familiar names; some of them, such as 'Spanking Sam,' were known to be uncrossable unless you were an exceptional athlete. Older boys would be on hand to haul younger ones out of the mud when they fell short. After much consumption of 'Pure' and 'Shandygaff' at the Red House, a favoured venue for rowers too, 'We were ferried across, black as ink, and with garments rolled in mud, teeth chattering and our hands and lips blue with cold. Once on the other bank we ran off like greyhounds to Dean's Yard, a source of mirth to the skies and shop keepers of the back streets about Westminster'. It was more than ritual humiliation: there were no baths in College.

The narrowness of modern team games and the habit of mind they generate seem a poor replacement for this range of self-originated diversions. But in the second half of the century, organised sport began to displace the older pursuits: more formalised athletic sports and football matches emerge in the 1860s, exactly when the anarchic excitement of the rowing matches with Eton, so disapproved of by authority, came to an end. The railway system made possible a new pattern of sporting fixture. There was a football match against Harrow in 1852, another against Haileybury in 1857, played in dense fog. No one knew who won, and it was never played again. Then in 1863 began the long-running fixture with Charterhouse. When the two schools persuaded the Football Association to adopt their off-side rule in 1867, and the modern game was launched, a kind of respectability is in the air, appropriate to a decade in which the Public Schools Act sought to give Westminster a new start. It is as if, having lost the old Whig families, the Byngs, Grosvenors, Pagets, Lennoxes, Pettys, since the 1830s, the School had to seek approval and custom from a professional middle class instead. In 1855, Terence's *Eunuchus* was dropped from the rota of Latin Plays, in deference to public taste.

In its own eyes, Westminster's superiority had never been in doubt. One of the most extraordinary features of its whole history is the maintaining of the illusion of greatness long after there had ceased to be any foundation for it, in intellect, or in conduct, or numbers, or the pre-eminence of its mature men. The races with Eton attracted quite as strong a following among the sporting gentlemen of London as the University Boat Race, and, despite falling numbers, Westminster usually managed a good race. In 1837 it is said that Westminster's victory led directly to the death of William IV, who had ventured from a sick-bed in the hope of an Eton success, and returned disappointed to his death-bed. Cricket matches proposed by Charterhouse and Shrewsbury were both loftily declined, the first because of the ungentlemanlike manner in which Charterhouse conducted itself in a match in 1796, the second because Westminster reckoned to play no schools except public schools: an elite of six names. Most Decembers the Latin Play attracted an impressive list of distinguished visitors, including William IV in 1834. His attendance had been secured, however, by a daring trick by Midas White, an Old Westminster and young roué who had been leading scholars into scrapes. Posing as the Captain of the King's Scholars, he talked his way into the royal presence and secured the King's promise to attend. Williamson was aghast, and made haste to gather a fit attendance: 'the more conservatives we can get about him the better', though the more confident expectation was that he would snore his way through the *Eunuchus*. The episode confirmed, though, that Westminster was a Royal school despite being in grievous decline. Had not the Scholars, and privileged Town Boys too, been present at every Coronation since 1685, and established the precedent of being the first subjects to greet the new monarch, with a cry of '*Vivat*'? Their presence and contribution on that first occasion is unlikely to have been designed; however, so great is the power of precedent in these matters that by 1907 Anson, in *Law and Custom of the Constitution*, had rationalised their presence as representing the populace, having rehearsed formally the part played spontaneously by the crowd in a medieval coronation. It is a claim which has been upheld at every subsequent Coronation, though not without strenuous efforts at the Court of Claims, which heard representations about the right to participate in the ceremony, in 1902.

An Earl Marshal's apprehensions are entirely understandable: the introduction of a phalanx of schoolboys is a severe test for even the finest organisation. At William IV's Coronation, they fitted well into a ceremony with a vigorously extempore contribution of cheers, hisses and groans from the congregation as the politicians, especially Grey and Brougham, did homage. 'I hissed with all my might', reported one Scholar in a letter home, 'and the Chancellor did not appear peculiarly well pleased as he showed by the twitches of his nose'. During the lengthy proceedings the boys lost interest, and were distracted by wine, buns and peaches bought for them by a kindly old peer from a refreshment stall set up in 'the Nunneries' the popular name for the Triforium based on the fantasy of a split level religious house for both sexes. At Victoria's Coronation in 1837 the boys were placed in the organ loft, though it would have been well if they had been banished from the Abbey altogether, noted a sardonic observer 'for a more murderous scream of recognition than that which they gave Her Majesty Queen Victoria yesterday was never before heard by civilised ears'. In 1902 their long wait was 'beguiled by agile youths performing mountaineering or acrobatic feats of climbing in the tracery of the Triforium and by one of the Rose windows, to the diversion of some of the spectators, to the horror and fear of a much larger multitude'. Then, perhaps because of a mistaken signal, they greeted the Lord Chancellor instead of the King with '*Vivat*' and, led by James Gow, the Head Master, gave an unrehearsed 'Three Cheers' to cover up a musical hitch when Edward VII emerged from the Confessor's chapel. Even in 1953 the Queen's Scholars were still eating lunch when they were supposed to lead the acclamations from the Triforium. It is hard not to recognise some justice in the suggestion by a teacher in 1953 that a group of children from other London schools would be more appropriate representatives of the nation's youth, though they would obviously need a great deal of rehearsal to make such an inspired muddle as successive Westminster boys. Perhaps that is their real role.

In 1883, when Charles Broderick Scott, resigned, after twenty-eight years as Head Master, weary, and anxious about an ailing wife, his letter to Canon Milman is full of regret and unconfident hope: 'No one knows as I do how far my work has fallen below even my own standard. Still some fruit has ripened – and I

Queen's Scholars being fitted with Coronation Dress in 1953.

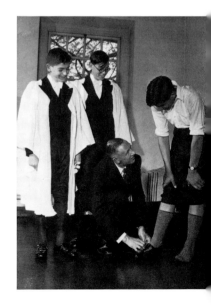

Ashburnham House in 1881. In
its last years as the residence of
the Sub-Dean, Lord John
Thynne. The original stone
porter's lodge and the high wall
flanking it give it a prison air; the
intention was to exclude
schoolboys. The upper storey
had been added some years earlier
to provide bedrooms and
servants' quarters.

trust and hope the old system may not be broken up and that the School may
continue to increase and no pretext be given for altering its character'. He is much
too self-deprecating, for he above all men made the revival of the School's
fortunes a possibility. During his time Westminster gained its independence from
the Dean and Chapter, steadily regained its pupils (he took over a school of 116,
and handed on one of 233), and dramatically and controversially expanded its
buildings. Above all, he preserved the structure and location of the School in the
face of strong contrary opinion.

In 1861 and 1862, the Public Schools Commission had held a series of meetings
to investigate the condition of Westminster. The Commissioners' report was
published in 1864, and the Public Schools Act followed in 1868. No one
connected with Westminster emerges with much credit. Liddell, now Dean of
Christ Church, repeats his opinion that there is no hope for Westminster as a
boarding school unless it removes to the country, objections to which he
dismisses as sentimental. The alternative is for it to become a large day school, and
cease to be a public school in the common sense of the word. Scott admits that

attempts to modernise the curriculum have failed, and his ignorance and ineffectiveness are exposed. He did not know of many College and School practices, such as the delegation of punishment for minor offences to Second Election boys; he acknowledged that orders he had given to improve the lot of Juniors had not been heeded. He admitted that College needed 'considerable alterations'. But time and time again the evidence indicts, openly or by implication, the Dean and Chapter. Thanks to the development of Tothill Fields the value of a canonry by 1862 had risen to around £2300 per annum. The Head Master's salary was £39, the Under Master's £15. The bulk of the income of the masters had to come from leaving fees, distributed as dividends. By this means the Head Master collected £1082 a year, the Under Master £569, and other assistants between £200 and £300. All the Scholars were kept for about £1200 a year, but had to pay in addition £34 each for tuition, washing, fuel for fires. The Chapter provided no furniture for them, nor any maintenance in Hall for the Under Master. As to the boys' food, though beef was served four days a week, and mutton three, the leavings from dinner were served up cold for supper in order of seniority. The Head Master played no part in Chapter discussions about the School.

The disdain and hostility with which the Reverend the Lord John Thynne confronts the Commissioners leap out from the transcript of the evidence. He was Sub-Dean and occupant of Ashburnham House, the Chapter's most prestigious residence, set in the midst of School buildings but defended by a forbidding wall. He had been a Canon of Westminster since 1832. There was no argument he did not use to evade responsibility. The original Statutes had never been signed; in any case they had never been kept; the Chapter were concerned only with the Scholars, and did not recognise the Town Boys; the establishment of the Ecclesiastical Commission in 1832 took the direct financing of the School out of the Chapter's hands: £1400 had been fixed as the annual expenses then, and there was no means of altering it. The Chapter had generously commemorated the Tercentenary in 1860 by providing a covered playground for the School (actually in the hope of diverting the boys from the Cloisters). There was no evading the figures though: from a Chapter income of £47,000 in 1861, £961 were provided for the School. Thynne was enthusiastic for the School's departure for the country.

The Commission left open the issue of the School's location, but the Public Schools Act of 1868 set aside a capital sum of £15,000 for the purchase of additional buildings when they fell vacant. Among these was the first option on acquiring Lord John Thynne's house upon his death. There relations simmered, while Lord John took what steps he could to achieve immortality. The School was independent, though the Dean was Chairman of the Governing Body, and the Chapter strongly represented. The incipient arrogance shown in the falsification of Chapter accounts presented to the Commission, was magnified after the Report was published. The Commissioners advised that a house should be pulled down, in the interests of air circulation: the Chapter rebuilt it on a larger scale; they urged that a building should be provided for the School and that College Garden should be more accessible to boys than the three days a year conceded at the Election: the Chapter ignored both recommendations. It endeavoured in 1867 to transfer estates to the Ecclesiastical Commissioners which would fix the whole future income of the School at £1400 a year. Meanwhile Scott set about internal reform: new regulations for discipline, to which boys were supposed to commit themselves by signing a promise in the Head Master's book ('no severe punishment, shall be used, except for grave moral offences such as falsehood, dishonesty, impurity, profanity, bullying, resorting to public houses or other improper places, drinking or smoking, contumacious defiance of authority, or breach of the rules after warning given'), a facelift for the curriculum (drawing or music for everybody, but only in time taken from play hours; a science lecturer from King's College two hours a week), attempts to reduce the self-infatuated isolation of College by making Town Boys eligible for scholarships at Christ Church and Trinity. He and the Masters unanimously supported the continuance of College despite its sullied reputation, believing it to be the prerequisite of Westminster's remaining a boarding school rather than being a day school, with the loss of what was distinctive about it.

In 1881 John Thynne died. As if stunned, the Chapter made no move. So Old Westminsters in Parliament carried, without a division, clauses expressing their pleasurable anticipation of the fulfilment of the appropriate sections of the Public Schools Act, and an acrimonious public dispute burst into life. The Dean and Chapter offered a much smaller house in Dean's Yard in exchange for Ashburnham, and then, wearing their Governing Body hats, accepted their own offer. Old Westminsters protested, alleging that the Governing Body no longer represented the interests of the School, and brought in the Charity Commissioners to block the transfer. The Chapter published a statement in *The Times*, expressing their relief at relinquishing the arduous and often thankless task of superintending the School. Flames were fanned by the airing of plans to demolish Ashburnham and to build a library, or fives courts, or private baths, or a chapel on the site. A Committee for the Defence of Westminster Abbey was convened, and Old Westminsters made an eloquent submission to Gladstone in return. But neither the law nor the School was to be diverted, and so it was that, in defiance of a renewed tide of feeling that Westminster should go to the country, 'the most conservative of all public schools', having decided not to demolish Ashburnham after all, spread out from its single Schoolroom after 284 years, and dug in its roots at Westminster alongside neighbours with whom it would have been impossible to be on more poisonous terms. It is not to be wondered at that, amicable as relations between Abbey and School generally are, the collective memory occasionally stirs.

'I wish my successor had been a public school man', wrote Scott to Milman in 1883. 'I fear the absence of this training will be felt.' William Gunion Rutherford's arrival at Westminster precipitated more than fear in his pupils.

> The coming of Rutherford was to us ordinary boys of the School like a terrifying cataclysm of Nature. After Scott's mild regime, Rutherford's fierce gusts of passion, his voice of thunder, his uncouth Scots rolling out reverberating 'r's, his restless flashing eyes, his long and purposeful stride, struck terror to us all. He seemed

suspicious of everybody, at enmity with every idea and custom to which we held. A crusader called on to cleanse; a man Carlyle would have loved, and whom to know throws light on Cromwell.

He was perhaps the first Head Master since Busby to carry the sense of greatness with him. His sudden visits to classes spread panic among masters and boys; he could reduce Seniors to tears by cross-examination in form. But if he was feared, he was also admired. He took a personal interest in each boy, and interviewed every boy once a term in a friendly heart to heart talk. He gave the impression of a man shaken by deep feeling as he prayed by the side of each boy in his Confirmation class, as if wrestling with the Devil for his soul. He was not interested in capitation fees, and kept the school to about 220 boys. He demanded high standards, and superannuated the idle; his leadership was morally and spiritually exalted, and he preached sermons of high idealism, establishing in his first year a morning service for the whole School in Poets' Corner as a vehicle for his vision. Sound financing was dear to his Scots heart: he was also the terror of the cleaners.

Such a man would have ruffled any institution; his impact on conservative Westminster was little short of apocalyptic. An ardent reformer, whatever he did would have upset boys and Old Westminsters, however necessary we now see his actions to have been. In his first year he founded a 'Modern side', i.e. a curriculum of non-classical subjects, but he also abolished rowing, taking advantage of a unanimous petition from the masters who felt that the journey times involved, since boys had to go some way up river because of its embanking, cut too deeply into their working hours. Old Westminsters were angered: they had recently hired a steam launch to carry boys up river from Parliament Steps. Next he abolished the old style Pancake Greaze, held every Shrove Tuesday. The whole school used to scramble for a pancake thrown by the College cook over the old iron bar in the Schoolroom, on which once hung a curtain to divide the Upper School from the Under School. The origins of this arcane and violent custom are uncertain, but Jeremy Bentham's reference to it in 1755 is the earliest firm evidence. Rutherford found it barbarous, and reduced the numbers involved to representatives of each form, a practice which still prevails, mercifully, in these days of 600 pupils and co-education. There had certainly been barbaric moments connected with it. In the 1830s, when a cook failed to get the pancake over the bar, he was 'booked' and then hunted through the Cloisters till he took refuge in his own kitchen. In 1865 there had been a memorable Greaze. A new cook failed to loft the pancake on either of his two permitted shies. A brute of a Welsh boy called Morgan hurled a Liddell and Scott, the heavy Greek lexicon, at his neck from close range. The panic stricken and enraged cook flung the pan into the mass of threatening boys, striking George Dasent on the head and opening up a gash above his eye. Blood flowed; the cook fled, and was instantly dismissed. A woman was appointed in his place. In the light of such episodes, Old Westminsters' representations that the Greaze was an outlet for animal spirits and a successful amusement for the School were of no avail: the event was brought within the pale.

The Pancake Greaze of 1919. The central group of spectators includes the Duke of York, later George VI, the Prince of Wales, later Edward VIII, the Dean of Westminster, Herbert Ryle, George V and Queen Mary. On the extreme right stands the Head Master, James Gow, in his last year of office, and almost completely blind.

Rutherford's major strategy, however, was to be a failure; his attack on College alienated everyone. He thought, with Liddell, that a boarding school in London was a complete anachronism, and was inclined to attribute the cause of its remaining in London to sentimental Old Westminsters. So he determined to push through his view of Westminster's destiny, that it should be a great day school. He neglected the boarding houses, and by 1894 there were only 31 Town Boy boarders to 156 Day Boys, in a school of 220. College was the centre of the boarding community, and the focus of Old Westminster loyalties, so he attacked its traditions of fagging and tanning, its monopoly of monitorships, the Election ceremonies, the structure of the Election system within the house, and sought to shift the Latin Play from the Dormitory to the Schoolroom. All this softening up was a preliminary to his proposal to abolish College altogether. Here was a hornets' nest indeed. The masters opposed him, because they did not share his aim of making Westminster a day school; they also valued a boarding education which was 'accessible to gentlemen of limited means' (the cost to parents of a place in College was about £30 a year). Old Westminsters, especially former Scholars, swarmed around a parliamentary caucus, and protested to the Dean, the Governing Body, the Prime Minister, vilifying Rutherford, defending fagging, tanning, the 'living constitution' of College, the entire status quo. Boys opposed him because boys always oppose change. The outcome was a compromise: College would remain, but twenty additional Day Boy Scholars were to be appointed. No doubt Rutherford hoped this change would dilute the strong brew of College, and in the forty or so years that non-resident scholarships were awarded, they certainly attracted many pupils of distinction, including Lord Adrian, Roy Harrod and John Gielgud.

This crisis past, Rutherford's energies relaxed: he came to feel an increasing respect for Westminster's traditions, which had proved themselves even stronger than he. In his last years he was much beloved, 'in his rustling silk gown like Olympian Zeus'. Worn out by his work, he retired in 1901, aged only forty-eight, having seen the School into the twentieth century. A former pupil saw him for the last time in 1906: 'though he was barely 54, his hair was white as snow, and he looked a saint'.

Rutherford had no apprehensions about his successor, who was also not a public school man. James Gow was a friend of Rutherford and a fellow Scot, who had practised as a barrister before going as Head Master to Nottingham High School, where he had raised numbers from 180 to 397, founded a cadet corps, and conducted affairs with a robust and practical, if ungracious energy. At Westminster he did precisely the same, and it was presumably what he was appointed to do. It was fortunate that two Scots should have given their country's skills to the service of Westminster at a time when it was imperative not to be trapped in tradition, gentility, dandyism, or financial slackness. Gow was an admirable antidote to all of these. He was a brusque, rough diamond of a man, with a broad provincial accent and often intemperate and abrupt in speech: 'I'll take yer gowns off yer back,' to Scholars who had done badly in exams, 'just hold yer row', or 'the

Pancake Day in College Hall kitchen c. 1900.

Westminster boys gathered outside Ashburnham House in 1903. The number on view represent about half the total school at that time. Sixty years earlier, the school had been reduced to half this number of pupils.

The rod table finds a new function: curiosity, apprehension, eagerness are all evident on the faces of what is presumably a modern language class encountering new technology Up School in about 1910.

boy's a fool' were his catch-phrases. He was short and thickset, with a grim expression produced by a drooping moustache and peering short-sighted eyes. 'Grit' and 'an uphill game' were favourite topics in his sermons, and it is probably fair to see his period of office as gritty in most respects. He was a humble-minded man, remote in manner, but full of robust common sense, and more genial and warm-hearted than his appearance suggested. At a break he liked nothing better than to pace about the yard, dealing briskly and honestly with problems brought to him by masters and boys as they joined him. He was dogged and self-reliant, particularly in business affairs, for which he had a natural capacity. In his first year he established a cadet corps, as many schools had done in the wake of the reverses in South Africa. By the time war was declared, all but sixty boys had joined it. During the war years, three parades a week took place, and uniform was worn by most boys every day in School. He also modernised the curriculum. Rutherford had taken little interest in science: up to the end of the century it was still taught to volunteers by occasional lecturers from outside the School. Gow immediately secured land to the south of the precinct, in Great College Street, and built a science block in time to teach science seriously to a generation of boys which contained both the future Lord Adrian and Henry Tizard. Little escaped his vigorous attention: renovation of the old buildings, drains, heating, classrooms, games. He abandoned Rutherford's day-school theory, and drew in more boys, many of them boarders. He also revoked his predecessor's ban on rowing, and the river at Putney was again ornamented with pink blades, the colour adopted by Westminster in the 1830s (to the rueful embarrassment of more fashion conscious recent pupils) in place of light blue, in deference to Eton's prior claim to that colour. His legal training stood behind his business acumen: he won important rating concessions for charitable institutions in a test case before the House of Lords. He was defeated only by the intransigence and tight-fistedness of the

College Hall in 1816 (*top right*), depicted in Ackermann's *Schools and Colleges of England*. The fire is still in its medieval position in the centre of the room.

Westminster from the Victoria tower (*bottom right*). The green roof of College and the red roof of Ashburnham House, centre left, mark the boundary between School and Abbey.

Ecclesiastical Commissioners when he attempted to get the 1868 endowment increased beyond its annual figure of £3500.

Many of the boys responded unsympathetically to Gow, or found him slightly ridiculous. The young gentlemen were exaggeratedly conscious of good form, and he had caused a stir by appearing at a football match without a top hat. We know a great deal about the attitudes and conduct of the boys from a diary kept by Lawrence Tanner during his year as Head of Grants (1908–9), a house of which his father Ralph was housemaster. The circle of Seniors who were his friends took themselves very seriously, organising and electing themselves to presidencies, secretaryships, treasurerships and committees of 'Deb Soc', 'Bug Soc', 'Shak Soc' as if they were already managing the affairs of the great world. They have preconceptions about style to which poor Gow and his like do not measure up. Tanner comments on 'one fearful person who appeared in tweeds (tweeds, think of it, at the Westminster play!) from University College'. They also took very seriously questions of discipline, and heard 'cases' at great length before passing sentence. Public 'handings' by the Head Master were still in use for boys who had disgraced the School, but each Monitor also had his own tanning rod in which he cut notches for every boy he had tanned. Reading the diary is exactly like reading the public school fiction of the time; one's perspective is unsettled by the discovery that what had always seemed to be a literary convention was probably an exact transcript of life and language, unless of course by 1908 everyday attitudes had become shaped by fictional models. Here is one revealing episode:

A dormitory 'Up Grants' in about 1908.

> The events of the day have not been uninteresting as during the morning B. Ward came up to me and told me they intended to have Tyson 'Up School' for having kicked the Green ball from opposite the Bursary down to College and also it hit Troutbeck as he came out, I also gather he has been somewhat of a nuisance in his house this term – Accordingly at 5 o'clock we the Monitorial all assembled in the VIIth room, and B. Ward explained to us the nature of the case and said he supposed we were all agreed that he ought to be 'tanned'. Clarke murmured something but was over-ruled. A knock at the door and the cane arrived which B. Ward holding in his hand told Edgar (the junior member of the VIIth has the duty of opening the door) to call Tyson who had been outside to come in. B. Ward with his back to the Table stood and faced him and said 'On Saturday afternoon about 2.30 you kicked the ball from opposite Ashburnham down to College' 'Yes' 'Well you *know* you mustn't do that' 'I didn't know' 'It is one of the commonest of School Rules. Have you any remarks to make. No. Do you wish to lay your case before the Headmaster. No. Take off your coat'. Voila tout. I didn't know a small person like B. Ward had such power of arm, he gave it hot and strong. Afterwards Tyson put on his coat with scrupulous care, B. Ward simply gazing straight through him with an icy stare until he backed to the door and slipped out. Then and not till then the tension was relieved and we gurgled with laughter. I told B. Ward as we came down that the exit was a masterpiece. It seemed so odd to be coming down and finding most of the School assembled outside the Houses and I had to 'process' across the Yard to where the Grantites were gathered around the steps. I tried to walk past without a flicker in spite of their broad grins. Marriott asked me if he had been tanned and also another coarser question. Under the circumstances and with his own fate (though he didn't know it) trembling in the balance I answered that the second was an illegal question and escaped into the House.

An autumnal view of Ashburnham House and Little Dean's Yard (*top left*), from the windows of Grants House.

Tothill Street in the eighteenth century (*bottom left*): an animated impression of street life.

It is only fair to Tanner, who returned to the School to teach history, memorably, for a short time before becoming Keeper of the Abbey Muniments for a lifetime, and one of the loyalest and best-loved Westminster figures of the century, to quote his own reflections on his diary, added in 1940:

> There was a general sense of security which the war of 1914–18 put an end to once and for all. We who were at School during the decade (1900–10) shared in that sense of security. We were neither thoughtless nor were we over thoughtful . . . we did not wish to reform the world, we were quite happy criticizing our own little world. We were unpestered by 'youth movements' and such like, and our duty to our neighbour was limited quite rightly to supporting (not very adequately it must be confessed) our own School Mission. . . . We had none of those 'obstinate questionings' which seem to entangle the modern boy. We never thought it wrong to exercise our authority. If, for instance, we beat a boy, we beat him because we thought he deserved it, because it was the recognised punishment for certain offences great and small and that was that; it was certainly not considered by either of the two concerned as a relic of barbarism or as indicating sadistic tendencies. The very real unhappiness in an unhappy world and the attitude of rather restless and critical discontent which seems to come to the modern thoughtful boy was not ours. We were content, perhaps too content, with our little world as we found it . . .

Few Westminster families could have escaped the experience of loss and grief, death and injury between 1914 and 1918. 216 Westminsters died in the war; more appear in the lists of wounded. There were only minor excitements, however, in the School's corporate life. Gow himself rang a bell in the Yard to announce an air raid and boys were sent to the Norman Undercroft beneath School; shrapnel fell; a shell landed in Little Dean's Yard, failed to explode and buried itself to be dug out four years later; Mrs Gow did the rounds blowing a child's trumpet to signal the end of a raid. But Gow also lost a son in the war and his health and his eyesight rapidly deteriorated. His last years were sad ones. Nearly blind, he either had to be led, or tottered round on a stick. Energies had gone; apathy prevailed. There was no zest or interest on the part of masters or boys. The buildings were cold and neglected; a staff mostly appointed in the previous century were sticking it out until replacements could be found after the war. To look at photographs of masters or boys of Gow's time is to confront images that seem very distant, rooted in Victorian England. Between 1918 and 1921 a phase of life, local and national, characterised by hierarchy, absence of self-questioning, unity of values, fervent loyalties to country, institutions, friends, seems to reach its natural end. The Unknown Warrior was buried in the Abbey in 1920; a School fund, opened in 1918, led to the unveiling of its own War Memorial by the Duke of Connaught in 1921. These two events conveniently mark the end of a predominantly aggressive, competitive, military, often brutal chapter of Westminster's story. Gow's last epigram at the Election Dinner of 1919 looked back, and asked for forgiveness for what he might have said or done to hurt people. A criticism of Westminster in the same year, that it had much less *esprit de corps* than other schools, is prophetic of a new order.

6

ZEAL FOR A CRISIS:
1919–1945

SOMEWHERE in the twenty years between Gow's retirement and the outbreak of World War II lie the roots of Westminster as a liberal school. The careers of John Gielgud, John Freeman, Angus Wilson, Tony Benn, and Brian Urquhart of the United Nations, suggest some aspects of a qualitative change, from tradition, conformity, classics, the narrowness of vision coupled with the unquestioned exercise of authority by boys over other boys conveyed by Tanner's diary, towards the arts, independence of mind and action, internationalism or at least political interest of a national and European kind. The consequence was that by the time Angus Wilson left the school in 1931, he could number, retrospectively, among its benefits 'a genuine liberal tolerance and friendly willingness to allow people to be stupid in their own fashion'. No single set either of events or personalities seems accountable for this change, which is perhaps all of a piece with the permanent effects of the war upon middle-class life and character.

The tension between change and continuity is a particularly even one in this period. On the face of things, many pre-war habits remain, and present a reassuring facade. Until 1939, Seniors still wear tail coats and top hats, Juniors Eton jackets and top hats. All boys, as a matter of course, carried umbrellas. The Latin Play reappeared, still a social event of absurd grandeur. Orders and decorations were worn by gentlemen, long dresses and long white gloves by

ladies, who continued to be segregated in a Ladies Pit, eighteenth century style. On one occasion in the 1920s, ambassadors, the Archbishop of Canterbury, the Speaker and the Prime Minister were simultaneously present, causing consternation about precedence. The small band still played, as it had done for most of the previous century, 'See the Conquering Hero Comes', as the Head Master and his party made their entrance. The Epilogues continued to manifest the triumph of ingenuity over wit, with '*Rumpant si declaro terrifico mi*', and '*Sileas. Ubi gannit*' being rendered 'Rum pants I declare, O terrific, O my!' and 'Silly ass. You began it'. The 'Mons Gods' still held captive his disdained and precarious ledge of small Town Boys at the back of the auditorium, holding aloft a tanning pole as a signal, and then waving it to and fro when he wanted them to applaud. The curriculum remained firmly traditional: only three of the twenty-five staff taught science, and only in Classics was an education of quality available. Sixty-three per cent of the boys, the Head Master was able to tell the Classical Association in 1924, still learned Greek. The structure of discipline held for a number of years: House Monitors and School Monitors still held 'courts', and tanned boys for a variety of trivial or at worst harmless offences, such as using an unauthorised route to Vincent Square (a house tanning), switching off an escalator in the Tube during a rush hour (a School tanning), or breaking an Abbey window with a rifle shot aimed at a pigeon, or convincing a Spanish assistante that smoking was allowed in class, so that the Head Master found teacher and boys all with cigarettes lit. For these last offences, the ultimate disgrace, a public 'handing' by the Head Master was imposed. The power of public disgrace, which seems to have vanished in recent years, also underlay public drill for bad behaviour, conducted by the uniformed school sergeant with a squad who had to wear special blue caps, like convicts. All boys were required to attend school matches as spectators, and it was a tannable offence to 'cut' before the game was over. Though safeguards against abuse of corporal punishment were introduced in 1923, such as the insistence on a regulation pattern of cane, on a maximum of four strokes, and on a boy's right of appeal to his housemaster before execution, the last of these rights was rarely if ever exercised.

In Dean's Yard a lamplighter made his nightly round, a horse and plough appeared on Green after the football season to assist with re-seeding, and some residents still rode out on horseback for an early circuit of the park. In the immediate locality, the elegant way of life evoked by Virginia Woolf in Mrs

Scenes from the thirties: two seniors talking at the meeting point of Little Dean's Yard and the Dark Cloister (*above*); breaking up for the Christmas holidays of 1936–37 (*below left*); spectators at a football match at Vincent Square (*below right*).

Dalloway was sustained: the Reiths, Trevelyans, Runcimans and Davidsons all entertained grandly, while a cricket ball's throw away, in Marsham Street and along the Thames, slum houses festered in silent shame, at least until the Thames flood of 1928 turned the public eye upon them. Cheap domestic labour enabled the Head Master's wife to run her house with a cook, a nannie, and six resident maids.

Yet across the warp of continuity run the new threads of change. A new young Head Master, Harold Costley-White, succeeded Gow in 1919, after only two energetic years at Liverpool College. He arrived to find three captured German guns presented to the School by the Government, already beginning to rust in the forecourt of Ashburnham House. Believing that they embodied inappropriate values, he determined to get rid of them, yet feared to do so publicly. So he conspired with the City's waste department and the Abbey authorities, and the guns were quietly carted off as scrap metal between 2 a.m. and 3 a.m. one morning. He also inherited an elderly staff, ten of whom, with three hundred years of service between them, retired equally quietly in his first three or four years. His freedom to appoint a large number of young masters was a crucial reinvigoration of a tired place.

Costley-White was a strikingly handsome man, of immense presence, authority and conviction. Richard Wollheim remembers him as 'large, silver-haired, highly mellifluous, somewhere between a bishop and a general risen from the cavalry.' He was musically gifted, often sang solos in School concerts, and a supporter of the first Robert Mayer concerts in Central Hall, which two hundred formally dressed Westminster boys would regularly attend. A classical scholar, like all Head Masters of Westminster until 1957, he loved teaching, chose to teach as large a timetable as he could, and often deputised for absent members of staff. Though circumstances compelled him to launch an appeal for a Games Fund early in his time, and though he had the good sense to appoint Donald Knight, the England cricketer, to the staff, he had no natural understanding of the sporting life. Seeing boys sitting about at a cricket match, he asked Knight what they were doing. Knight explained that they were either out or else waiting to go in. 'Oh', said Costley, 'can't you find them some work to do?' But he was essentially a kind man, whose interest in and care for the boys always led him to put them and their interests first. He set the lead in altering the nature of relationships between adults and pupils. He stepped in to end the institutionalised bullying of junior boys.

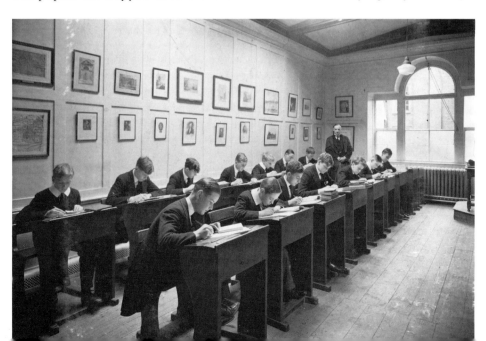

A class at work in 1933, presided over by A. T. Willett, Housemaster of Grants. The room, to the east of 'School', is fourteenth century in origin, and was used as a small dormitory by monks claiming the privilege of a fireplace.

Second year Scholars, for example, were no longer licensed to beat their Juniors for a range of trivial offences, such as walking on the wrong side of the stone pathway across the Yard. He also invited boys of all ages into his own house for breakfast, lunch, tea and supper parties, and if games of 'Clumps' in the drawing room after tea seem to us as an improbable way of entertaining teenagers, we must bear in mind that it constituted a revolution in relationships in its time, and that there was no distinct subculture of their own to make boys critically conscious of adult devised party games.

He was open-minded enough to sanction a school ballet in 1931, on which masters and boys, led by H. S. Williamson, later Head of Chelsea College of Art, had eagerly collaborated, cheerfully resisting the hostility of the sporting faction, and the widespread conviction that it was a decadent activity for school boys. 'A nice, plucky boy, but please! he should get his hair cut', Costley-White wrote of one boy, not realising that he had grown his hair long in order to take part. The argument that profits would go to the School Mission was used to convince the uncertain. Though there were no profits, no-one seemed to mind. It was judged a great success, and was reviewed enthusiastically by *The Times*.

Although in 1919 there was still underlying gloom about the future of Westminster as a boarding school, and even continued talk of a move to the country in order to preserve the status that boarding gave, Costley-White believed none of it. He set about making the School better known, bringing in a wide range of visitors to stay in his house and see the School. His own wider interests, particularly in PNEU (the Parents National Educational Union), of which he was Chairman, and the English Speaking Union, through which he worked to establish transatlantic exchanges of staff and pupils, gave him an international platform from which to broadcast Westminster's name. He attacked the dingy neglect of the buildings that had set in during the war: chocolate brown paint and dustbins yielded to white paint and chandeliers. Boarding numbers rose, so first a waiting house had to be created and then in 1926 a new boarding house, Busbys, initially at 6 and 7 Dean's Yard, part of Markham's terrace, and later at the east end of Herbert Baker's new Church House. He acquired seventeen acres of land at Grove Park, in the southern suburbs, for the expansion of sport.

External events too began to influence the attitudes of the School. Costley-White had arrived during a rail strike; seven years later, the nine-day General Strike made Dean's Yard a day and night depot for Government messengers, with tents pitched on the grass. Boys were allowed to volunteer for strike duties as long as they had their parents' consent. Some worked in the ticket office at St James's Park station, others at the Lot's Road power station. John Carleton, a future Head Master, was given twenty minutes instruction and then asked to drive a tram between Shepherd's Bush and Hampton Court. One evening, he fouled the points, derailed it, and was relegated to conductor for the rest of the strike. The History VI worked to get copies of *The Times* out at Printing House Square, where Barrington-Ward (O.W.) was assistant editor. Though boys leapt at the chance of some fun, the strike seems to have had a lasting effect on the consciousness of a privileged class. Throughout the Thirties, there is a deepening of political and social awareness combined with a quickening sense of crisis. The General Strike,

Latin prayers in 1933 (*left*). The picture clearly shows the indignity of trussing to which the hammer-beam roof had had to be subjected and the columns of family names filling every remaining area of stone surface. Latin prayers Up School in 1986 (*right*).

the Slump, the growth of Fascism, even the Abdication issue served to externalise boys' interests. In 1931 John Bowle, then a young History master, founded a Political and Literary Society, which was visited in its first year by Gandhi and, in quick succession, by Harold Nicholson, Attlee, Baldwin, Bertrand Russell, Auden and Toynbee. In 1936 a radical pacifist society, the United Front of Progressive Forces, or 'Uff-Puffs', was founded. Its aim was 'the formation of a wide People's Front similar to those which have achieved such splendid success in France and Spain'. It flourished for over a year, and numbered nine masters and about a quarter of the pupils in its membership. There was consternation among Old Westminsters, who inveighed against this Bolshevist scandal. A United Front song opened meetings; branches were established at Oxford and Cambridge, peace rallies were attended, and a weekly paper published, all in the interests of 'uncompromising resistance to reaction, militarism and Fascism'. Wollheim recalls Peter Ustinov in the back of a football bus debating the Brest-Litovsk treaty with Rudolf von Ribbentrop, whose father was German Ambassador, and who gave the Nazi salute to the chauffeur of his official white Mercedes as it brought him each morning to Dean's Yard. He was, by all accounts, a friendly and popular boy. Towards the end of the surviving minute book is the entry: 'only one thing can kill the U.F.P.F. and that is a big war which will blow Westminster and the U.F.P.F. to blood and ashes. And that is what the U.F.P.F. exists to prevent'. It collapsed in 1937, stricken by internal divisions, about the Abdication, and between Marxists and moderate Leftists, and also perhaps having expended the enthusiasm that had fuelled its idealism for a few exciting months. Loss of vigour is not the same as apathy, which was blamed in 1937, as on many subsequent occasions, for the failure of Westminster endeavours. The cycles of change and fashion are very rapid in a school, like speeded up film of a growing plant. The Uff-Puffs may have been impractical, but they were not unrepresentative. The Corps was disliked, but, though technically voluntary, was difficult to evade. The hectic, over-charged mood of 1936 and 1937 was compounded by a financial crisis. Many schools had to tighten belts in the 1930s; Westminster without any capital endowment was especially precarious. Austerity was personified by Bursar Tyson. He would have no secretary, typewriter or telephone, and persisted in keeping even the coal for the Bursary fire locked in the safe. A more practical reaction to the crisis was the formation of the Westminster School Society, to set up and administer an endowment fund for the School's benefit. It was a step that seemed prophetic of the needs that lay ahead. Costley-White, stricken by a series of thromboses, resigned in 1936 and, after a short period as a Canon of Westminster, was appointed Dean of Gloucester. On the day he left Westminster for the West, 28th September 1938, Hitler invited Chamberlain to Munich. As the Costley-Whites drove out of the precincts, they passed Westminster masters loading up lorries for the School's first evacuation to Lancing.

At Christmas time in Coronation year, the new King and Queen came to the Latin Play. Three and a half years later they were again in Westminster, to sympathise with an empty and partially ruined school. The events of that period are so bewildering and improbable that months, or even days, replace decades and years as the narrative unit. Even those most involved find the sequence difficult to credit: it is a story that deserves a fuller re-telling than is possible in a book with a broad canvas.

In August 1938, John Carleton, then a young master, on holiday with a Westminster family in Yugoslavia, heard that the Coronation Chair had been moved out of the Abbey. He felt that this action was decisive, and returned home quickly. Shelter trenches were being dug on part of Vincent Square. The new Head Master, John Traill Christie, the first lay Head Master since Camden in 1598, had an agreement of many months standing with Rossall, near Fleetwood, to evacuate Westminster to Lancashire in a crisis, and all the practicalities of such a move had been fully prepared. The European situation deteriorated in September to the point at which war was hourly expected, and evacuation essential. On 25th, Christie made public his plans for Rossall in a circular to parents, asking for their consent for a move which could occur at five minutes notice. Luggage labelled 'Rossall' was ready to go. The issue of this letter led to a summons to the War Office at 1 p.m. on Tuesday 27th, where Christie was told that Rossall was requisitioned by the military. He now had either to disband the school, or to find alternative accommodation within twenty-four hours, for the move had to be made on Wednesday 28th, after which the School would lose its buses. Christie telegraphed Lancing, where the Head Master, Docherty, was an Old Westminster, and sent John Carleton to Sussex. 'Get into your car and find somewhere for us to go'. Carleton was rebuffed at Ardingly, but received sympathetically at Lancing. 'When do you want to come?' asked Docherty. 'Well, tomorrow, actually.' Docherty summoned Lancing's lady caterer. 'Miss Saunders, three hundred and sixty Westminster boys will be arriving tomorrow.' 'Oh yes, Headmaster. About what time?' 'About five-thirty', said Carleton. 'Will they have had tea?' she asked. Her face suddenly clouded. 'There's just one thing', she said. Carleton waited in apprehension that everything might go wrong. 'We're rather short of spoons.' He returned late on Tuesday night to report room for the

A platoon of the Corps parades in Dean's Yard in 1937 (*left*). King George VI and Queen Elizabeth visited the Latin Play, the *Adelphi*, in December of their Coronation year, 1937 (*right*). Here they stand on the stage to greet guests, accompanied by John Christie, who had become Head Master in the same year.

hundred and fifty boarders at Lancing and Hurstpierpoint. The next day, 28th, a new circular was sent to parents, temporarily disbanding the day boy section of the School. Luggage labels were changed, and at 3 p.m. that afternoon, boarders were taken to Sussex by bus. Everyone was greeted at Lancing with the news that the crisis was over, the war off, Chamberlain at Munich. Christie shrewdly decided to stay for a few days. Indeed, anxious about losing his day boys to other schools, by 6.30 p.m. he had found room at Lancing, camping out in an empty farmhouse, for as many day boys as had wished to go to Rossall. They were contacted, and instructed to come down by train on 29th, while masters and wives ferried seventy-two mattresses from London, and in six hours dug latrines and prepared the farm for feeding and housing sixty. It was a short stay, but a good practice. Day boys returned to London on Saturday 1st and Monday 3rd, boarders were collected by bus on Tuesday 4th, and Westminster resumed in S.W.1. on Wednesday 5th October. Christie had to justify the disruption and especially the expense of the exercise to the Governors on the same day. He also had time to write an alphabetical jingle for his staff.

> A's our alarm at the danger of war
> B are our Buses packed up at the door . . .
> K is for Kitbags so full you must cord them
> L is for Lancing – may Heaven reward them!
> M is for Murray, and Marjorie too
> N is the number of things they can do. . . .
> Y is the Youngsters we tried to restrain
> Z is their Zeal for a crisis again.

Christie now had to make new plans for a more permanent evacuation. Estate agents were quick to send details of large, empty, semi-ruinous properties. The search was wide: the West Country, Derbyshire, Scotland; the Earl of Lonsdale telegraphed 'Suggest Lowther Castle Penrith If Emergency Again Accute [sic]'; Sir S. Maryon-Wilson, Bt., D.L., of Eastbourne, wrote from Yattendon House to offer accommodation for fifteen to twenty scholars accompanied by a master, plus the use of a small private theatre: 'I do not wish to have what may be described as "slum" children quartered on me'. Nothing suitable emerged; the success of the Lancing experiment encouraged everyone to think of repeating it. There were other distractions. It took six months of patient negotiation with the City Engineer's department to get the Vincent Square trenches filled in so that the ground could be used; no sooner was that accomplished than a letter stamped 'SECRET' arrived, beginning 'I have the honour to inform you that in the centre [sic] of your cricket ground in Vincent Square has been selected as a site (No. 5/32) in case of Mobilisation, for one Balloon of No. 905 Balloon Barrage Squadron. It is found that billets for the crew of ten men could be conveniently arranged in the School Cricket Pavilion'. The theme of the Epilogue of the Latin Play in December, the last of its kind, was gas masks.

At Easter 1939, the Italian invasion of Albania seemed to make the next move imminent. Christie wrote to housemasters: 'Hostilities may be upon us before the end of the holidays. 300 boys can go to Lancing and Hurst. If war breaks out, and I can't telegraph, come straight to Lancing (and not via London). With more than usually warm wishes for a restful holiday'. Instructions to parents included 'Top hats should not be brought'.

During August 1939, Westminster was packed up and moved to Sussex ready for the new term. Houses were rented in Shoreham, and billets arranged in private houses, to take the overflow of boys whom Lancing and Hurstpierpoint could not house. Christie was installed by the end of the month, and wrote to the Bursar in London 'I think there's nothing for me to do but sit tight somewhere in Sussex, answer letters, and receive evacuees, till we know if its peace or war. Hitler and Musso are in a funk!' September 3rd resolved the uncertainty and term began in Sussex on 20th September. The school retained its own identity, and settled down happily to new routines, which included bicycling to Brighton, filling in ration books for Worthing R.D.C., rowing on the Adur, and knitting for the troops, for which gratitude was expressed to 'the girls of Grants'. Between December 1939 and May 1940, the executive level considered the future. Lancing was felt to be a short-range policy; now a long-range one was sought. The alternatives to remaining in Sussex were to move somewhere else and unify the school under one roof; to become a different kind of school, simpler, more self-reliant, better adapted to a post-war future; to return to London and be 'the real Westminster again'. Safety, independence, finance, the supply of day boys all had to be juggled. The decision in principle that was taken, to return to London, was the worst possible one and ironically led directly to Westminster's becoming 'a different kind of school', by necessity rather than by choice. People who were assumed to be in the know either allowed their judgement to be swayed by sentiment, or revealed the blindness of Government expectations. Lord Davidson was in favour of a return to London. Church House was an ideal air-raid shelter. 'The defences of London are increasing in strength every day, and unless the Hun goes completely mad, it seems incredible that he would be so foolish as to attempt large-scale bombing . . .' Lord Sankey also advised a return to 'a unique locality and the tradition of centuries'.

Westminster boys gathered in Vincent Square in 1938, during the Munich Crisis, to watch the first barrage balloon rise from its anchorage. Shelter trenches were dug in the square at the same time.

If the idea of a return to London, fed early into the collective consciousness, was quixotic, the failure to reappraise it in the wake of May 1940 was indefensible. Lucie Christie saw the sea covered one night with tiny moving lights, and woke to find exhausted men sleeping in the gardens of Shoreham villas. The Dunkirk rescue suddenly placed Lancing in the front line of an expected German invasion. New plans had to be made for an emergency evacuation, to Hurstpierpoint by lorry, or over the downs by bicycle and on foot, to village halls, outhouses, tents, anywhere. Iron rations were laid in. John Carleton was sent to Exeter, where a short-term refuge was available in Reed Hall and Mardon Hall, two University Halls of residence. Timing was perfect. The Regional Defence Commissioner gave Lancing and Westminster a week's notice to leave the area on June 20th, the day the students in Exeter dispersed. On the same day, boys with bicycles were instructed, in the event of an enemy invasion and advance, to travel towards Horsham, with light luggage and a groundsheet, there to bear west and make slowly for Exeter, avoiding towns and main roads. After a musical competition on the evening of June 24th, two hundred and fifty Westminster boys and one hundred bicycles were taken from Shoreham by special train to Exeter. A suitcase containing £150, kept in readiness for distribution to boys in the event of invasion, flew open and spilled its contents on the platform. The rest of the term passed in ease and glorious sun. There was a regatta on Elizabeth I's canal; Michael Flanders and Donald Swann first appeared together in a revue in aid of St David's Church; the teaching staff, including Christie, patrolled at night as Local Defence Volunteers.

The Governors had decided that Westminster would return from Exeter to Westminster for the autumn term, though the staff felt nothing but apprehension at the prospect. Only thirty new boys had sent entry forms for September, and twelve of those would not come unless the school were back in London, and the Governors obviously felt that indecision was bad for morale and for recruitment. So in August, furniture was moved back and unloaded; hundreds of yards of blackout curtains were made by voluntary squads of masters, wives, and boys. The last bed was moved in on September 7th. The next day the Blitzkrieg began. Term was indefinitely postponed, and for the next two months the school was homeless and dispersed. Six masters lived continuously in Little Dean's Yard, keeping a round-the-clock rota of fire-watching, using the stoke-hole as headquarters, playing darts and drinking tea, and sleeping in the undercroft cellar of the Rere-Dorter, which they shared with the Head Master and a number of maids known, innocently, as 'nymphs'. The atmosphere was that of a school dormitory, with Christie as monitor. 'Mrs Kerr, where are my pyjamas?' he would ask, or, when one of the nymphs refused to lie down, 'Mrs Bluett, won't you adopt the prone?' She didn't understand him. Other masters came in from the country for relief shifts; some informal teaching was attempted, in an effort to hold the day boys. Meanwhile, six other masters, plus Christie himself, scoured the country for a new home. An attempt to return to Exeter was frustrated by the prior claim of the Royal Free Medical School on the laboratories there. The plight could not have been more desperate. 'The longer we wait', wrote Christie to the Vice-Chancellor of Exeter, 'the more our boys will drift away'. The financial crisis was deepening as borrowing had to be increased. Should Westminster be suspended for the duration of the war rather than risk utter insolvency? Go to All Souls? to Crichel in Dorset? Appeal to the National Camps Corporation? Petition the King? Christie did his best to reassure parents that something was afoot. Thirty houses were investigated; all were found to be scheduled for military use. At last, in the first week in October, some encouragement began to arrive from Herefordshire. Two masters, Preedy Fisher and John Carleton, sent appraisals of a dispersed group of buildings in a six mile circumference near Bromyard: Buckenhill, Saltmarshe Castle, Whitbourne Court and Rectory, Clater Park, Fernie Bank, Brockhampton House, and local farms. 'Large gardens, a pond with fish in it and a trout hatching place. A complete sawmill and carpenter's shop with a lot of forestry work undertaken. A smithy and workshop. There is water, but it is reputed to run out in summer.' There were difficulties, but no alternatives, and so the difficulties had to be confronted. Two of the houses were semi-derelict: masters and works staff laboured on them for most of October. Saltmarshe Castle had been ear-marked for Red Cross use, and so could be used only temporarily, and only for teaching; moreover, the owner, Mr Barneby, was difficult and erratic, sending telegrams such as 'Butler ill must put you off'. He wrote to the Dean after one unhappy meeting 'Unfortunately I suffer from a very quick temper and unruly tongue, and doubt if any further direct negotiation with Mr Christie is advisable'. Buckenhill and Whitbourne Court were both scheduled by the War Office: Wilfred Eady had to use his influence there to get clearance. Nothing conveys the fantasy of those days as well as his reply, part of which runs 'I hope the school will be able not to insist upon the wearing of tail coats at the week-end. The local peasantry will be somewhat startled. Moreover carting about top hats under present transport conditions would be a nuisance'. During October, forty lorry loads were packed up and driven to Bromyard by masters and works staff. On 28th, Christie could at last circularise parents with details; the masters met at Saltmarshe on November 6th, and the term finally began on November 11th. Grants boys brought a hundred hens on the point of lay by train from Dorset, which substantially deferred the first egg. Two hundred and fifty people had been inserted into Bromyard and neighbourhood where Christie had been told 'there literally was not a bed to be had'. It was as well to be in the country. In October the Busby Library had been destroyed by an incendiary bomb, and on the night of 14th, Miss Mecey, Christie's secretary, had been killed in an air raid while sheltering in Church House, the building identified as ideal protection for the School.

For the next five years, a whole generation of Westminsters settled into country life. They never knew Westminster-in-London except for holiday pilgrimages to be shown the place, and occasional plays put on in College Hall to affirm continuity. The School had been well prepared by its recent nomadic life for the transformation of its routine, and the reassurance of a home of its own was all the sweeter for boys being diffused between seven different houses, non-institutional as in Westminster. At 9.15 each morning, boys converged on Saltmarshe, by bus, bicycle, and on foot across the fields. 'The way from Saltmarshe to Buckenhill takes one first down the back drive and through a muddy farmyard; then steeply

Evacuation 1940: boys *en route*
to Sussex (*top left*); harvest camp
(*top right*); trying to
make Buckenhill habitable (*far
left*); leaving classes at Saltmarshe
Castle, near Bromyard
(*left*).

The Hurstpierpoint section of the
evacuated addressed by John
Christie in 1939.

The ruins of College Dormitory
after the air-raid of May 1941
which also destroyed School.

down to a brook crossed by a plank bridge, and up the other side to a field from which the farmer apparently tried to deter us, first by cows, then by carthorses, and finally by a bull.' A great part of life was lived outdoors. Three acres of kitchen garden was developed for food. In 1941 the gardeners with justifiable pride list their crops: 4000 lbs of potatoes, over 1000 lbs each of beetroot, tomatoes, carrots, 952 sticks of rhubarb. 'Chick Soc' delivered eggs and meat; there were bees, geese, ducks, a goat and Molly, a pony, for transport. Grants became 'a pig club', and received rations of pig food on condition that half the produce went for general use. Thousands of hours of work were given to local farmers, in harvest camps, and in fruit picking. Wooding for fires, local home guard duties (though the war seemed very remote), skiing to Bromyard for bread when the lanes were snowed up, cross-country running on Bringsty Common (a name still brought once a year to Wimbledon Common for a cross-country relay), rowing at Worcester. If team games suffered, societies and plays flourished, especially to give shape and interest to week-ends. An old stable was converted into a music room housing fifty people, and an ambitious programme of concerts began, with local people cycling miles to come and play. There was Shakespeare in village halls, there were folk dancing classes and displays; the Corps and Scouts were both more fulfilled in the country. Photographs and letters are full of cheerfulness. A House duty list reads: 'Pigs Hens Coal Lamps Acetylene Engine Wood Boiler Rabbits and Blackout'. The difficulty of finding and keeping adequate staff made it as well that such an alternative education was available. For all the anxieties over water supply, the cosseting of temperamental 'Ram' engines, the digging of wells, pleading for petrol and water carts, there was joy in the water that you had toiled to provide. Despite inadequate teaching and equipment, these are acknowledged to have been wonderful years. Christie conveyed why in a circular letter in 1943: 'they gain just what such boys chiefly miss, contact with the earth and the countryside, whether they are digging potatoes or harvesting corn, or bicycling to school through acres of fruit blossom; few schools can have been so healthy for over two years as we have been'.

There was little attempt to retain old ways. Tails were worn on Sundays, because they had to be worn out; the Foundress was Commemorated each November in Bromyard Church. The Head Master made his base first in the King's Arms, Bromyard, and then in a cottage in the High Street. The Bursary alone remained at Westminster, with a visitors' book and a small maintenance staff. In the course of the war houses were let to the London City Mission, a Salvation Army canteen, the National Fire Service, Toc H and the War Department. Government cement was tested in the laboratories; American officers relaxed in Ashburnham House, re-christened The Churchill Club. On May 10th, 1941 a massive incendiary raid aimed at Parliament gutted School and College; Ashburnham House, and 17 and 19 Dean's Yard were saved from incendiaries which struck them and started fires. Old John Angel, loyal servant of the school for years, and chief tosser of the Shrove Tuesday pancake, arrived as usual for work to find the ruins. 'Whatever will the Bursar say?' were the only words adequate to convey his horror. A messenger was sent to Herefordshire, with the news that was impermissible by telephone, which seemed as unreal in blossomtime as the destruction of Coventry viewed from Bromyard Downs, impersonal, remote and strangely beautiful, the sky dazzling with searchlights and 'flaming onions'. There was an even rarer beauty amid the destruction in Westminster: a pair of black redstarts hatched two broods in a hole in the stonework on the stairway to School in the summers of 1940 and 1941, allegedly the only nests of the species ever recorded in London. The birds reappeared after the war, in the plaster moulding of the restored Busby Library, pecking at pomegranates; no visitors' book for them.

Despite the buoyancy of the young in Herefordshire, those responsible for the School were burdened with anxiety. In the first winter in Bromyard, rumour abounded in the Home Counties. The School had been wound up, was done for, was financially ruined; even, so much does rumour beget rumour, that boys had

The black redstart nesting in the bomb-damaged school buildings in 1941 (*above*), and commemorated in the restored ceiling of the Busby Library, 1951 (*below*).

been drowned in a basement by a burst main. It was hard, in wartime, to attack these rumours. Christie wrote a series of eloquent pamphlets from exile, affirming the School's spirit ('we are doing nothing less than starting a new school') the feelings of thankfulness and relief with which it would return to the city, his faith in the future of a city school with ancient traditions, and a balance of boarders and day boys. 'I would not have anyone suppose that we shall forget the town by being in the country, or that we shall return to Westminster with any feelings but those of thankfulness and relief.'

But it was increasingly hard to stay confident as numbers dwindled and one by one the outlying Herefordshire houses were vacated in 1942 and 1943. As day boys left, of course, there were no replacements, and the recruitment of boarders, except from the most devoted governors and Old Westminsters, was almost as impossible. Christie was found one day in his office in Bromyard, head in hands. 'If we go below a hundred, we're finished.' Then, cheering, 'Even if I have to wander the country with only the King's Scholars at my heels, I'll keep Westminster alive somehow.' A proposal to move to Harrow in 1942 was seriously considered; an Under School was courageously started in Little Dean's Yard in September 1943, to protect the existence of the Upper School, to meet educational demand in London, and to move some staff back on to the Westminster site as a bridgehead. The Governors recognised the pressures to return, and from 1943 were continually setting target dates which passed with the School still rusticated.

VE day came. There was a bonfire at Buckenhill, with Hitler as the guy. At Whitbourne, the boys used the drainpipe route, well practised on forays to cherry orchards, to slip out and join the crowds at the bonfires on Bringsty Common. Then there were farewell parties at both bases. Lucie Christie recalls, 'We invited everyone, the butcher, the baker, the candlestick maker. My ragged cobbler friend appeared in a suit with a flower in his buttonhole, and Colonel Lutley, much our grandest neighbour, said it was the nicest party he had ever been to'. In July and August, a removal firm ferried the portable part of the School back home, leaving behind only Mr Claridge, who had turned the Library into a thriving little bookshop in a disused public house, and decided to stay and run it.

Three hundred and seventy boys had left Westminster in 1939; one hundred and thirty returned. The war years had been financially crippling. The annual deficit in the late thirties had been £5000, and the overdraft £19,000. In 1945 the debt was £67,000 and the gutting and neglect of the buildings made the total loss by the end of the war around £400,000. Because of its unique position, it suffered more from movement, losses and damage than any other public school. Yet the benefits of the war years, though not quantifiable, probably compensated: a qualitative and permanent change in the character of relationships, from the hierarchical to the companionable, from a team to a community spirit; the broadening of the idea of education beyond the classroom, the social importance of involvement with local life, and the shedding of a great weight of tradition, of minute but obsessive distinctions and anachronisms which proved unfit for travel. And, since none of the pupils who returned in September 1945 had ever known Westminster at Westminster, there was another new school to be started.

7

DEAR LIBERATED ONE:
1945–1986

As the story moves into our own time, inhibitions throng in. Personalities and events have not attained the reassuring permanence, or seeming permanence, or the curiosity of historical objects, nor have they become misrepresentable by anecdote. Many leads from the post-war cast are still living, or are cherished in memory by relatives and friends; unworthy truths are, or must remain concealed for the time being or for ever. Besides, the important trends and truths are unlikely to be yet apparent to any eye. Yet a bland catalogue of events can make only tedious reading, so some judgements must be attempted, though necessarily provisional, and perhaps of most use as a sounding board for historians of the future, who may find our narrow vision comic.

It was just as well that the School had shrunk to a third of its pre-war size, for there was no room for more in the battered buildings. As it was, communities had to play follow-my-leader during the years of reconstruction round the houses which still had roofs. There were no classrooms and no College; lessons went on in the house rooms, and the scholars moved into the pre-war Head Master's house. School was a shell but could be used for assemblies on dry Wednesdays and as an open-air rifle range. The Churchill Club continued to occupy Ashburnham until December 1945, a solace only to masters grateful for admission to secure drinks untasted for six years. A brick air-raid shelter stood in the middle of Little

In June 1946, the School held a garden party in College Garden (*left*) to celebrate the return to London. The shell of College in the background is a reminder of the School's desperate state in the post-war years. The first Pancake Greaze after the war, in February 1946 (*right*), took place in a roofless School. Here a section of the damaged Greaze bar is tied in place ready for the event.

Dean's Yard; the corps had to drill round it. Vincent Square was unfenced, a battleground for local children, and littered with the dismal residues of war, shelter trenches, static water tanks, American army trucks and barrage balloon anchorages. For three years, field sports all battled at rather than to Grove Park, the Old Kent Road being less traffic-choked than it became during the sixties. For two or three more years finances were precarious. Christie cancelled all cricket fixtures in 1946 on the grounds that the School couldn't afford them. The crisis arrived in 1947; the new Dean, Alan Don, declared that Westminster should not sink beneath the waves during his Decanate, and immediately a sharp rise in numbers argued his prescience or his proximity to the divine ear. John Christie himself, worn by the strains of war, was ill from time to time until his resignation in 1949, and the School was deprived of his decisive leadership at a crucial time.

Little of all this clouded the mood of the School as it settled with long-awaited relish to reoccupy its heritage. An air of excitement and challenge prevailed, stimulated by the process of reconstruction. A wide range of activities and skills were quickly under way, for the war years had shown everyone how to make do in rough and ready conditions. The wartime vigour of Arnold Foster's music was unabated, and the catholicity of country life reappeared in activity or culture afternoons, inspired by John Carleton, when forms and form masters disappeared in pursuit of Wren Churches, the Roman Wall, or London markets. Francis Rawes, who knew Westminster as a master before the war, briefly, and returned after it, was struck by the shift of mood. Before the war an ageing staff tended to consolidate the old ways. Black ties were still preferred for dinner parties; a mode of formal superiority was embodied in the old style Latin Play. The boys were, on the whole, self-conscious, complacent, also rather superior. The Scouts were the

focus of an anti-Corps clique (and contained both the Benn brothers), but 'we're not the Gilwell Scouts, you know'. Junior Debating Society, of which Tony Benn was secretary, met in Lord Stansgate's house. After the war there was a rapid intake of younger men to the staff, as after the first war, and though there were some odd temporary appointments (a geographer who only showed pictures of film stars, for instance), a succession of talented refugees – Adolf Prag, Ernst Sanger, Hugo Garten – added quality and versatility to a common room enriched by English graduates themselves broadened by war service. The boys had changed too: the changed relations and social attitudes fostered by their war experience were implicit in the abandonment of the old formal dress (simply not available, so no decision was necessary), and of all but the most nominal vestiges of fagging. Other houses, especially day boy houses, were challenging the pre-eminence formerly claimed by College and Grants alone. 'We're here, and we're different' was the general mood; the mannered elegance of the pre-war years was replaced by a good-hearted, more boyish naughtiness. At least two

99

Herefordshire practices continued. College evensong in Whitbourne Church resumed in St. Faith's Chapel, and Lucie Christie went on keeping chickens, by Liddell's tree and in Ashburnham Garden, and making jam. So when John Christie one day found himself in a headmaster's nightmare when he beat the wrong boy, he was able to offer his wife's new jam by way of apology.

The priorities and decisions of the Reconstruction Committee are difficult to fault. Within the limited recompense of the War Damage Commission and the School's own straitened circumstances, their plans made much sense. They decided to sub-divide Burlington's Dormitory rather than restore it, but to restore the Busby Library exactly, only with the addition of the redstarts. They decided not to build a 'Play Chamber' as a venue for the Latin Play, and not to build classrooms in Ashburnham Garden. They decided to roof 'School' temporarily and, when it was fully rebuilt in 1958–60, the last of the buildings to be tackled, not to replace the hammer-beam roof. The staggering of the work gave each year a new interest, a new excitement. After many stone picking parties, Vincent Square was reopened in 1948, a victory against the covetous gleam in Local Authority's eye, though a rearguard action against an under-

College Dormitory as it has appeared since its rebuilding after the war, with the blind windows on the first floor glazed. It is a sign both of changing attitudes and pressure for space that a building which originally had two floors in use now has five; the number of pupils using it daily has risen from forty to two hundred and fifteen.

ground car park had to be fought as late as 1964. So by the time John Christie resigned to go as Principal to Jesus College, Oxford, in 1949, recovery was both assured and far advanced. Though not a natural administrator, he had led Westminster through its most cliff-hanging years, and ensured its survival; though a shy and unspontaneous man, he had presided over a transformation of its relationships and its attitudes. But he was tired, and needed release.

Another classical scholar (and perhaps the last), Walter Hamilton, followed Christie as Head Master. An aloof man, with a sombre, lugubrious and endearing wit, his *obiter dicta* are still cherished. 'Nearly the end of term, Head Master'; 'Twenty-five days', he would say with gloomy precision, as he looked forward to his escape to the simple pleasures of the countryside, and especially the Isle of Mull, which were central to his existence. He arrived a bachelor, and departed a married man; indeed his departure after seven years to be Headmaster of Rugby was prompted partly by a wish to bring up a family more spaciously. His celebrated proposal – 'My dear, how would you like to see my name on your tombstone' – must be apocryphal, but is so true to the man that, like the best Busby stories, it will not go away. He began by trying to found an inappropriate tradition, by announcing that boys were to acknowledge him with a sort of salute as they passed, but the request was quietly buried after he found that, curiously, he never passed any boys. He continued by questioning traditions that were established. He was opposed to the resumption of the Latin Play, terminated the

College was re-opened by George VI in 1950 (*left*). After the ceremony in College Garden the King and Queen cross Little Dean's Yard with Walter Hamilton, Head Master, and John Carleton, Master of the King's Scholars. Football returns to 'Green' after the war (*right*): a photograph taken about 1950.

101

ceremonies of Election at the end of the summer except for the Election Dinner, held again from 1953. He threatened to terminate the triennial Commemoration of Benefactors, the Latin service in the Abbey which seems to be a relic of pre-Reformation England, but which was actually instituted by Rutherford in 1889. Though Hamilton struck some of his colleagues as philistine, taking little overt pleasure from or giving little overt encouragement to art, music and drama (he didn't want more than one play a year), he was appreciated by many as an academic consolidator rather than as an innovative or imaginative Head Master. At unendowed Westminster, numbers in the school are more than usually determined by financial needs. Though the number was set at three hundred and eighty in 1950, the largest it had been since 1746, (except for one term in 1933), applicants began far to outnumber places, and so the entrance exam became a competitive rather than a qualifying one. Hamilton built on this popularity, exacted high standards, and so by 1955 Westminster outstripped all other schools in terms of awards won at the ancient universities. He also achieved a surprising amount of expansion with limited resources: a new boarding house, Liddells, in 18 and 19 Dean's Yard; a new Under School in Eccleston Square, after an intractable wrangle with an unsympathetic neighbour, Canon Smyth of 20 Dean's Yard, who could reconcile himself neither to the return of the senior school nor to the replacement of the Head Master by a shrill Under School in 19 Dean's Yard. He wrote indignantly to the Church Times in 1951: 'If a century ago the School suffered from the Abbey, the boot is now upon the other foot'. The episode briefly sent bad blood circulating again between the neighbouring institutions, and an advanced plan for an exchange of sites, Ashburnham Garden for part of College Garden, where a new science block was proposed, was rejected by the Chapter at a late stage. Finally Hamilton set about the rebuilding of Grants, 'one of the worst structures we have seen in any school in England', the Inspectors said in 1951.

The decade was particularly law-abiding nationally, and Westminsters too behaved responsibly, for the most part. Hamilton was the last Head Master to be largely untroubled in this corner of his empire. The magazines of the time convey a worthy though rather dull stability: a range of respectable societies, holding regular meetings, and still compiling minute books; grey-haired and motherly matrons 'recommend Clydella' on the back cover of the *The Elizabethan*, and a major news item at the very limit of daring is the flying of a housemaster's pyjamas from the Abbey flagpole. It was as if the excitements of the previous decade had disposed the place for a quiet and purposeful enjoyment of its renewed life and buildings.

John Carleton, a boy at the School in the 1920s, a junior master in 1932, Master in College from 1949, was appointed to succeed Hamilton in 1957. His preferment echoes the long Westminster lives of men such as Busby, Knipe and Vincent. It was a bold appointment, and he was a unique Head Master. For one thing he was not distinguished academically, and made no secret of his lowly degree. (His Oxford years had been financially precarious: with no assurance that his widowed mother would be able to pay the next term's fees, he had sensibly concentrated on mastering the Westminster Abbey material in the Bodleian rather

How did they get through the arch? This detachment of Horse Guards seem to have lost their way. The date is 1967.

than the texts prescribed by the History School.) He was everyone's chum in the Common Room, a compulsively sociable man, one of the young bachelors who had played bridge on the pavement in Barton Street before the war, and had made merry as he, supremely, knew how. On the one hand an eighteenth century figure with patrician manners, very much at home on a Grand Tour, with civilised interests in art and architecture; on the other hand he was utterly without side, was universally affable and hospitable, and had a twinkle in his eye for everyone. Lawrence Tanner was his friend and mentor; together they knew everything about Westminster, School and Abbey, and both published books about it. No one was better fitted to understand, to defend and to disseminate the heritage. He could not have been a headmaster anywhere else and would not have wanted to; and, indeed, he would not have been taken for a headmaster by anyone with preconceptions about the breed – but possibly as a member of the royal household. He was as likely as not to interview aspiring members of staff over dinner at the Garrick Club, and I remember vividly my first evening in Westminster, and my first encounter with him. He had a new Ford Zodiac, and shot away from the lights in Parliament Square at about 60 miles an hour. Waved down by a policeman on a motor cycle somewhere near Downing Street, he first winked at me, then wound down his window and played a favourite role, a muddled, incompetent and utterly innocent Wooster: 'Frightfully sorry, officer;

Annually the first VIII rows from Putney to Westminster, disembarking at Black Rod Steps and taking tea in the Palace of Westminster in recognition of the long established right of Westminster boys to pass through the Palace to reach their boats before the embanking of the river and the increase of commercial traffic made rowing at Westminster impossible. This wet arrival took place in 1960.

brand new car – had no idea about the acceleration – terribly stupid of me'. Released with a reprimand, which he took like a crestfallen schoolboy, he winked at me again, and we sped off to the Garrick.

As adjutant to John Christie, after the School's return from Bromyard, he had been much involved in the bread-and-butter work of reconstruction, both of the buildings and what went on in them. As Head Master he had the opportunities to improve and embellish his estate, in the manner of an enlightened eighteenth century landlord. Dinner-parties at No. 17 often ended with a conducted tour for his guests through the glories of Ashburnham House and the Greene Library, then by the Dark Cloister into the Abbey, mysterious in moonlight. He used his charm ruthlessly to secure appropriate gifts to the School: the Purcell organ, pictures, Restoration chairs, curtains for the rebuilt School. When the Westminster School Society wished to commemorate his headmastership, he characteristically chose a fountain in Yard: a lack that he had never felt quite able to ask the Governing Body to supply. These things gave him personal pleasure; far more, they were to help create that civilised atmosphere that was such a part of what Westminster offered – where the past was present but never overpowering, and there were standards of elegance and seemliness for those who cared to notice. His inexhaustible interest in people, his wide range of acquaintances and his Westminster instinct combined to make him a shrewd judge, when appointing masters, of those who would find the School to their taste. He was seldom wrong, and so was able to resist a headmaster's chief temptation, to interfere, because he knew that if he gave staff and boys freedom and encouragement, the School would seem to run itself, while he could stand back and enjoy it, enormously enthusiastic and characteristically self-deprecating. He may have appeared an amateur, but he was thoroughly professional. He was skilful in his handling of the Press – London headmasters are particularly vulnerable to their attentions – and here his wartime work with S.O.E., when many of his colleagues were journalists, had given him useful experience. At the dinners and other public occasions on which Head Masters have to hold forth, he was a relaxed and entertaining advocate of Westminster. He sometimes used these occasions to counter the notion that Westminster was not very interested in science: pointing to the number of Westminster F.R.S.'s, to the new science laboratories, and to the creation of the Tizard Lecture which honoured a scientific O.W., Henry Tizard, and attracted a series of distinguished speakers. When the great Cultural Revolution swept through the ranks, and youth became permanent rather than transient, culturally, linguistically and morally separated out from maturity, Carleton was an ideal man in charge. He may have been as bemused, and felt as helpless as other headmasters, but he was readier to be amused than panic-stricken, standing back to take a historical perspective, citing the appalling behaviour of the past in order to put the present into perspective and refusing to label states of affairs as problems unless they really qualified. He was quick to defend the boys against their detractors, especially letter-writing busybodies. In letters he was able to deliver sharp and witty rebukes without forfeiting sympathy, so perfect was his manner. Someone had written to complain of the boys' appearance, particularly their long and dirty hair. He read the letter to the

School in Latin Prayers, and then his reply, part of which ran: 'It is no more logical to equate long hair with dirty hair than it is to equate long legs with dirty legs'. Yet he did not shrink from coruscating censure of individuals who, in his view, were bringing Westminster into public disrepute. There was no avoiding a sense of crisis, though, between 1968 and 1972. Relationships between masters and boys came under strain, because usual signals did not arouse usual responses. A successful housemaster gave up his house, because he no longer felt able to manage. Boys went into huddles, and looked blankly at adults; the atmosphere was one of furtive ferment. Undoubtedly there was a drugs epidemic, and the naivety of adults provided both the safety of virtual immunity from discovery and the danger of unrestricted experiment. There were new sights to be seen. In an odd schoolboy interpretation of radical gestures, would-be rabble rousers wore pyjamas in breaks, and harangued audiences from the wall in Little Dean's Yard. Yet Carleton's equanimity and detachment, and the fluidity of Westminster were better fitted to absorb such challenges, which seemed more alarming at the time than they really were, than schools that were more self-contained, and on a shorter leash. There was a great deal of discontent, some unhappiness, and a few spoiled lives, but not many. Carleton's benign and avuncular presence soothed passions that a more overtly managing Head Master might well have inflamed. His touch was put to the test one evening when a group of modern 'skies', leather-clad, armed with chains and knives, appeared in Little Dean's Yard and struck an aggressive posture. The area suddenly emptied of everyone else. John Carleton, taking his ease on his roof garden, spotted them, and sallied out, armed with a pipe and a cravat. It was like the final confrontation in the deserted main street of a one-horse Western township. He strolled across, unperturbed by their baleful stares, clicked his tongue in the familiar way he had as a prelude to friendliness, and said 'I say, you really shouldn't be here, you know'. They hung their heads, and allowed him to shepherd them away. It was an epitome of his attitude to 'the troubles'.

There was, perhaps, little 'development' in the usual sense of the word in Carleton's time. Much embellishment, much exercise of taste applied to his love for Westminster, much living out a civilised life in privileged surroundings as its own end. His own sense of the place had been fashioned before the war, and radical policies were neither needed nor expected. He had an able staff, and many talented pupils. So he was the least likely figure and, in context, the one best placed to achieve without fuss, as radical a change as any in Westminster's history, the arrival of girl pupils followed naturally by the appointment of women to the teaching staff. Such a break with tradition, for which his successor is generally held responsible, occurred in October 1967, as an informal arrangement with another school. It was a perfect way to initiate a process that developed so gradually that there was no one point at which a clear decision had to be taken or a clear issue emerged to divide people. 'An experiment which may be terminated at any time', was Carleton's line. He never even informed the Governing Body until the first generation of girls was established in the School. But when he resigned in 1970 to enjoy a retirement that was to be all too short, it was obvious to all that girls were more than birds of passage.

Westminster had never given its pupils many targets to attack. One exception was the Corps, which took hasty cover one afternoon when some dissident seniors fired an air rifle at the parade from a Dean's Yard window. Not long after, the Corps was abolished, after a brief life as a voluntary unit, and what might have been a major source of hostility and ridicule disappeared well before the excitements of the late sixties. John Rae, who arrived in troubled times, could easily have been a target. Like John Carleton, he was no scholar, despite his doctorate; unlike him, he lacked the assurance and instinctive judgement acquired from a life interwoven with Westminster's. He had never been a housemaster; his experience of headmastering had been brief; his background was provincial rather than patrician; he had a wife and six children to install in the far from spacious Head Master's residence. But he established from the start a masterful public manner, and through the years of a headmastership more controversial outside the School than within it, his vulnerabilities shrank into insignificance.

Rae's years were also the years of inflation, and it became rapidly obvious how little manoeuvring space the School had. The professional middle classes could no longer be relied upon to provide the core of the School's pupils, least of all the Old Westminsters among them who, through lack of either disposition or cash, provided no more than about three percent of its pupils, in contrast to the over forty percent of sons of Old Etonians who stuck to family tradition. London was still affluent, but the affluence had shifted to a more cosmopolitan executive and managerial class whose notions of success, though perhaps narrow and specific, unavoidably determine Westminster's success, or even survival. As inflation galloped away, the School, heavily dependent on fee income, had either to raise its fees disproportionately, or increase the numbers in the School. But there was no room on a crowded and historic site to build, no resources sufficient to buy at S.W.1. prices. Besides, for much of the seventies the hundred and twenty year succession of headmasterly jeremiads about the future of boarding seemed at last to be coming true: boarding was out of fashion, and not just at Westminster. But at Westminster, one boarder had to be replaced by two day boys in order to preserve income. Schoolmasters' salaries were such that it was impossible to attract staff of sufficient calibre for an academically ambitious school unless accommodation could be provided for them, yet raising cash for this accommodation was not a cause, however worthy in itself, to touch the hearts or pockets of likely benefactors.

These inter-related problems provided the themes of Rae's period of office; they were not of his choosing, but were forced upon him by a threatening conjunction of economic forces with Westminster's local circumstances. His responses to them display a consistency which is clearer and more controlled in retrospect than often appeared at the time. His policy was not only consistent; it worked. Against the odds, he left Westminster a better known and more successful School than he found it. More even than that, he prepared the School for the future. He saw the importance of ensuring a supply of good entrants at the age of thirteen and of generating wide support through finance and goodwill, as a bulwark against hard or politically changeable times. The purchase of a new building in Vincent Square for an enlarged Under School, and the creation of a

Opposite. The Scholars in 1887 (*top*), gathered in the Deanery Courtyard and in 1983 (*bottom*), in College Garden. It has become traditional for a light-hearted photograph to be taken after the formal one.

Development Office, both owe much to his vision. Both ventures have already been fruitful.

The nub of this policy was the achievement of the highest possible academic standards. Westminster had always done well by its ablest boys, but was always open to criticism for not stretching the rest. If good results for all were what the market demanded, it was a demand that most public schools had to be seen to defer to. Rae, aided by the rise in importance of A-levels and the withering away of the old system of awards and entrance to Oxford and Cambridge, engineered a shift away from the closed society of an academic elect, especially in subjects such as Classics and History, to an acceptance of the necessity of doing as well as possible by every pupil. Though there were internal battles about emphasis, and accusations that Rae was undermining 'real education', the only serious loss was a narrowing of the curriculum to the purely academic. However, there were gains of a non-academic kind, such as the provision of compulsory outdoor expeditions twice a year for every boy in the lower school, the value of which was surprisingly recognised by a man who was wholly urban himself, and had no interest in distinguishing between a buttercup and a daisy. 'I thought we could get away with it a little bit longer', said the Clerk of Works one day when a library ceiling fell in. A mischievous critic could offer this as Westminster's motto in recent years. The School did 'get away with it', despite manifest deficiencies, because results were right.

The quality of these results was achieved and sustained by girls, who from 1972 had to be full members of Westminster School rather than bona fide members of another school. As always in the recent history of private education, an economic necessity and an academic advantage was represented as a general educational ideal. Up to forty girls a year were selected for entry to the Sixth Form, from a large number of applicants; they were talented, competitive, and rarely secured anything less than high A-level grades. A process that Carleton had initiated evolved of its own accord, and needed little further design or steerage; at no one stage was there anything substantial enough to oppose. However difficult many girls may have found it to adapt to Westminster ways, however unsatisfactory the ratio of the sexes, however much heartache was caused to girls and boys whose bids for social and sexual shares were rejected, the important truths are that the girls sustained academic levels during a period of expansion, and completed the process initiated in the late sixties, of youth choosing to occupy its own cultural and social territory rather than one staked out by adults. The arrival of forty new girls a year was only one part of the expansionary tendency which was the plain man's response to inflation. Perhaps the School might have been bolder in raising its fees, forgetting about its charitable origins and its traditional indebtedness, over many years, to the professional middle class; and it might also have judged both that there was still a lot of wealth about, especially with many mothers resuming careers, and that there was consequently more of a market for Westminster's weekly boarding system than there was for boarding in general. But the solution adopted was to increase numbers, sometimes by design, and sometimes by accident. Between John Rae's arrival and departure, numbers rose from 464 to 640. The deficiencies of this policy were a deterioration in quality of

life through over-crowding, increased wear and tear on nerves and buildings, and the failure to provide compensatory structures of care, instruction and discipline, let alone compensatory space. The advantages were that the expansion compelled a revitalising of the Common Room without prejudicing the positions of older members of staff, and not only expansion of subjects taught, but also the protection of both old and new subjects, with small followings, such as Classics and Russian. The difficulties created by this expansion were largely absorbed by the assumptions Rae inherited from Carleton, that staff knew how to approach one another and their job in a civilised fashion, tolerant, humorous, sympathetic, hardworking, professional without fuss.

John Rae was not a practical man. No-one had ever seen him even boil an egg. He had little interest in bricks and mortar, or such phenomena as timetables, which he happily left to specialists. Not much building was possible anyway, once the last Little Dean's Yard sites had been developed in a minor way under strictest controls. Yet he saw the importance of investing in the Under School, and gave it his full support, not only to underpin Westminster's main entry at age thirteen, about which anxieties lurked, but also to bring primary schools into the catchment area for Westminster with an intake at age eleven. It made good business sense with just a hint of idealism thrown in.

For some years yet, two views of Rae's headmastership will belabour one another until they merge in an exhausted, objective, unimpassioned peace. In the

The teaching staff
of Westminster School,
1908 (*above*) and 1986 (*below*).

blue corner, Rae the successful publicist for Westminster, eager to broadcast the name of the School, to keep it in the public eye at a very competitive time; Rae the accomplished educational politician, consummate on public occasions, which he loved, a man who enjoyed his experience as intrinsically political, as every successful headmaster has to some degree; Rae the man of stamina, tireless in the volume of work he undertook, whose love of this work stimulated extraordinary reserves of energy in him, and who remained on top of things because even the wickedest boys collapsed first; Rae the natural administrator, in his element at meetings and committees, master of paperwork and procedure; Rae who was fascinated by people, and good with them, who knew all his pupils by name and most of their parents on sight, who was around at all hours, talking, playing Yard cricket, bowling in the nets, as informal as his personality permitted, the dominant and ubiquitous presence who loved Westminster's incomparable living space, its collegiate sense, recalling Oxbridge colleges in former days, where teachers and students met pleasantly in the evenings.

But Rae himself, the most honest, self-critical and humorously self-appraising of men behind the urbane manner, would be the first to recognise the opponent in the opposite corner: Rae the self-publicist and scorer of own goals, who needed to be the centre of attention; Rae who was so political that he lacked spontaneity and who was so uneasy in the presence of emotion that he avoided confrontations with colleagues and pupils, and whose natural gesture in conversation was always to step backwards; Rae who used administrative thoroughness to defer or evade decision and actions; Rae who was addicted to films, and took little apparent pleasure in any of the other arts.

There is truth, though at present exaggerated truth, in both these selections. Icon within the School, iconoclast outside it, his double self is explicable in terms of insecurity, the preposterousness of finding himself, almost by accident, Head Master of a great school, and having to play out the role for all he was worth. His two defensive planks against criticism were to run a school that was unquestionably successful, and to make himself a public figure, as if in compensation for his lack of academic record. His love of public events sprang partly from their affirmation of the headmaster's centrality; he also welcomed the feeling of excitement such events gave him, the psychological, quasi-religious bonding from which modern headmasters tend to be excluded by their infrequent classroom appearances. A parallel excitement arose from his attraction to risk. Living dangerously was part of his fun, and if he sometimes burnt his fingers, others were pained more sharply than he was. He liked difficult deadlines, and having to rise to and surmount problems of crowd behaviour; he relished the irresponsible or provocative act, particularly at solemn gatherings such as the Headmasters' Conference. Something in him chafed at propriety; he was more in sympathy with the naughty pupil than the virtuous one, and understood boys and girls in trouble, as if he saw in them images of the irresponsible figure he once was, still wanted to be, and occasionally became again when he yielded to the temptation. He was at his best in the middle of the last night of term, when he joined a rota of masters on watch, not really because it was always necessary, but because he enjoyed the suddenly informal companionship of his colleagues in a kind of fantasy atmosphere, the implicit identification with the provocative members of the School, the game of cops and robbers over the roofs, dealing with mischief-makers in their own spirit. His 'Houdini mentality' seemed to spawn appropriate situations for him to relish. There was the highly accomplished practical joke of the removal and concealing of the Greaze bar the week before Shrove Tuesday. There was the breakdown of the van bringing the whole Election Dinner from Eastbourne, of all places, so that high dignitaries who included, that year, the Archbishops of both Canterbury and Westminster had to be plied with sherry for nearly two hours. While others scurried in panic from late-opening supermarket to Chinese take-away, John Rae savoured the sense of crisis. But he was also fascinated by the day to day routine of relationships and problems, and was entirely happy to expend the bulk of his energy in attending to them. For him, the ebb and flow of the School was the interesting thing; visions, plans and schemes the less interesting, a region of value chiefly as a means of sharpening the appetite for the daily drama. Westminster was the right school for him, as it has been for others who have stayed: men and women with breadth, diversity, a liking for city culture, and the humour and humanity without which the hurly-burly of daily life would be insupportable. If it attracts adults who possess the same spectrum of qualities no matter how often the individuals change, it also fosters in its pupils a comparable spectrum of qualities: sociable, not easily abashed, individualistic, detached and critical but capable of extraordinary efforts of creativity and co-operative effort, amazed and rather disappointed when rules are discovered to be applicable to them, adept at humoring adults, loyal to and concerned about one another. An anonymous message from one to another on a postcard of a Modigliani nude found in a library book perfectly captures the mood:

> Dear liberated one, here's crazy again. Its Wednesday, and I have temporarily Platonic prep proceedings to pen this to you. Yesterday I finished my Phillimore. Phew! What a weight off my mind. 'Once upon a time there was a tiny GIANT' do you remember that, Elaine? It cropped up in your hymn book, yes, your hymn-book. Anyhow. The 1st night of my play is tonight and I should be nervous. I bet I bugger something up violently. Wish me luck. Hope you are well and happy, if not, 'cod-pieces',
> Love Big Bad Bazz.

It reflects a way of life that not all will like. In their number will certainly be some who were moved to protest when Rae appointed Lynda Stuart – both a girl, and black – as Head of School in 1985: 'If I had a boy at Westminster I would withdraw him immediately'; and 'A grotesque distortion of the natural order of things'. Others will find it attractive in its honesty, and in its refusal to take itself too seriously. Mrs Thatcher had no comprehension of it when she drafted a special message for the Political and Literary Society in 1975: 'It is a time in which we must all make extra effort to safeguard the future of our Nation. It is a time in which each of us must shoulder our responsibilities . . .' Not yet, O Lord, not yet. John Carleton understood it perfectly, and it is fitting that the last word on it should be his: 'It is strange that schools should pride themselves on their antiquity when they can pride themselves on their perpetual youth'.

Westminster is the only long-established school of metropolitan origin that has adapted to city life rather than fled from it. Its distinctive character is rooted in that single fact. Staff and pupils are caught up in the ebb and flow of the town: there is a fresh tide, and the sense of a new start, each morning. There can be no bounds; narcissism and claustrophobia are largely avoided by the dissolution of the School into the city each day. Scholars retain privileged access to the Public Gallery in the House of Commons; the First Eight rows each year from Putney to Black Rod Steps to tea in the new Palace of Westminster, a reminder of the days when boys established a right of way through the old Palace to reach their boats. A circuit of St James's Park is a favourite ten-minute run, the shade of its trees attractive locations for more private pleasures. More evenings than not, groups of boys and girls are out on the town, at the Barbican or the National Theatre, the Coliseum or the Festival Hall. Art, English and History can take in the Tate or the National Gallery, the Banqueting House or the British Museum, in the course of the day's timetable. If cultural experiences of a more demotic kind tend to be restricted to weekends for the under eighteens, the prejudices of teachers must be held responsible. By virtue of its clientele and its location, Westminster is much more a prey to fashion than other schools, yet the range of experience available to those who will admit it supplies much more than a corrective. By virtue of its ancient site and buildings, and its continued links with Abbey and Parliament, it could appear to be imprisoned by tradition. Yet the very reverse is true. Where tradition is continuous and ubiquitous, it is taken much more for granted, as part of the processional order. And it is in the fine balances of fashion and tradition, of life within the Abbey precinct and life beyond it, of naivety and sophistication, that the metropolitan quality of Westminster is most clearly identifiable.

8

THE SCHOOL BUILDINGS

Most of the School's present buildings were not designed and built for the purpose of education. Yet they compose so satisfying an environment, of so many different periods, materials and associations that it is tempting to conclude that Westminster was fortunate in being able only rarely to purpose-build. They have a life and a history of their own, of which the School's use of them is only one part. And to their independent life they might one day return: the School does not even own most of them, but holds them on reverter leases from the Ecclesiastical Commissioners in which body Chapter properties were vested in 1832. Another eccentric feature of the buildings, rooted in the nineteenth century settlements, is a division of use and responsibility with the Dean and Chapter. In College Hall, for example, the Chapter pays for upkeep; the School has absolute rights of user during term time, but on the first day of the holidays, control reverts to the Abbey. The idea of a boundary is inappropriate. The Abbey is responsible for the surface of Little Dean's Yard, which is entirely surrounded by School buildings; there is a single cellar, about 24 feet long, half of which is technically the Abbey's, half the School's. Confusion seems endemic. In 1692, Thomas Knipe, Second Master, was 'almost poisoned with the stink' of a broken sewer, and feared the Chapter would not repay him for having had it mended; in 1718, the Dean was in favour of the Dormitory's being built in College Garden, but the

A view of Dean's Yard from the south-west corner in 1845: a lithograph by C. W. Radclyffe.

Head Master, Robert Freind, opposed it. Complications of use and of history threaten confusion too, in even a short account of the principal buildings, about all of which there are crucial uncertainties which even the rich storehouse of the Abbey Muniments has not yet resolved.

College Hall   Until the Dissolution, College Hall was the Abbot's state Dining Hall, the west side of a semi-fortified house built around a small central courtyard directly below the south-west tower of the Abbey. Together with the Jerusalem Chamber immediately to the north, it was the jewel of Abbot Nicholas Litlyngton's great building programme, and was completed in 1376 or 1377, when it was glazed. Henry Yvele and Hugh Herland, the mason and carpenter who also collaborated in the building of Westminster Hall, are believed to have been active in Litlyngton's service. The Abbot signed the building: shields held by angels forming the corbels bear his arms. Originally College Hall had a central fire on a raised octagonal hearth. This medieval practice continued until 1847, when it was almost certainly the last surviving example. The lantern in the roof was louvred for the release of smoke. Before 1847, College Juniors were made to leap over the fire; one, Charles Longley, later Archbishop of Canterbury, fell in, and bore the scars till his death. The musicians' gallery is Elizabethan and so are the tables at the side of the Hall, though there is not a shred of evidence for the attractive story that they were built from Armada timber. The painted coats of arms on the north wall

114

The same view in 1986.

behind the high table are of 'the three royal Colleges': Westminster, Christ Church and Trinity, and of the Order of the Bath. Here Elizabeth Woodville and her younger son, Prince Richard, took sanctuary in 1483, and here, after the Dissolution, the whole College of St Peter dined together, perpetuating the monastic brotherhood until the Prebendaries began to discover the pleasures of private life in the early seventeenth century. Here too the Scholars performed their early plays to Queen Elizabeth and the Council, on a stage in front of the gallery. It is still the home of the Election Dinner, first held in 1561 for the visiting Electors from Oxford and Cambridge, at which the speaking of epigrams by pupils on given themes provides an entertainment with the port which conflates the old collegiate practice of Saturday performances by Scholars, and topical comment in the epilogue to the Latin Play.

In earlier days, Dean's Yard was an open space only about half its present size, and was known as The Elms. At the south end, both in front of and on the site of what is now Church House, stood a cluster of buildings comprising the monastic farm, which remained until the eighteenth century, degenerating into a tangle of alleys and hovels. The Granary, with a gateway surmounted by a tower at its north end, was a long narrow building that ran parallel to the surviving monastic buildings on the east side of the yard. In exceptionally dry summers, the lines of its foundations appear on the grass. At right angles to it on the west side stood the

Dean's Yard

115

Brewhouse, supplying small beer to the College for centuries. Its work was impeded neither by the Reformation nor by the Commonwealth, the only known corner of the establishment to survive both events. The long range of buildings on the east side of Dean's Yard, which preserve much of their medieval appearance, were built, like the Granary and Brewhouse, by the indefatigable Litlyngton for monastic officers – the Cellarer, the Treasurer and the Monk Bailiff – and for Guest Houses. It was to the ground floor of one of the centre houses, number 19, that the School first moved into the precinct from the Almonry, probably in 1461.

William Markham won the consent of the Chapter to clear away many of the old farm buildings, and to build a grand square, largely for the benefit of the School. The old stone of the Granary was used to build a raised platform on which rose, between 1757 and 1759, a rather austere terrace of houses, some of which were used as lodging houses or boarding houses until their demolition to make way for the new Church House (1937–40). One older building, known as the Scholars' Coffee House, projected into Markham's square until 1815, when a second wave of clearance occurred. It is an attractive feature in the sketches and water colour done by William Capon in the last year of its standing. The School's use of the enlarged Green as a playing field was endorsed by the Public Schools Act, no doubt to the regret and anger of many subsequent residents and motorists.

Little Dean's Yard A vaulted passage, now known as Liddell's Arch after the house which, since 1956, occupies the Litlyngton buildings above, leads to Little Dean's Yard, like the main artery to the heart. 'Yard' was once just that: a narrow cobbled lane, still marked by a ribbon of small square white stones, along which the boys ran the gauntlet of high garden walls to the areas of private houses in order to reach the Schoolroom. These buildings, as randomly placed, it now seems to us, as flotsam on a sandbar, were gradually cleared away in the course of the eighteenth century, to leave the present stagey space stared at by over two hundred windows. The honey-coloured flagstones on the east side originally lined Burlington's open piazza on the garden side of College Dormitory, and were moved to Little Dean's Yard in 1847 when the colonnade was turned into election rooms. The enclosure of Yard bestows on Westminster the gift of civilised leisure: the fastest pace is that of pupils late for lessons, its natural inhabitants sitters in the sun; from it traffic can scarcely be heard, and no building be seen which asserts a twentieth century scale, while to the north the Abbey spreads a protective wall.

Gateway The classical gateway carrying the arms of Elizabeth I is by Burlington, and cost £283 18s. 1d. when the bill was paid in 1737. It marked the completion of his great work at Westminster, the Dormitory, and was intended as an entrance to both the Schoolroom and to College, which were to be connected by a raised walk. The names carved on it, and on the walls that line the steps beyond, reflect a passion of the middle years of the nineteenth century, when boys paid Abbey stonemasons to come in and cut their names on the stonework of School and College, in family groups in the one (Waterfields, Phillimores, Williams Wynn), in Election order in the other. Those who could not afford masons drove nails into the floor in the form of their names. The portico at the head of the stairs and the ornate doorway which leads on from it are both usually overlooked by residents

It doesn't look like a school: (*left*) the battered and grimy archway from Dean's Yard which has been the School's main thoroughfare since 1599 when the monastic dormitory became the Schoolroom. An eleventh century capital (*right*), formerly an external window of the monks' dormitory, now hidden beneath the floorboards of a modern classroom.

and visitors, but both were provided by Busby in 1680 or 1681, and somehow survived wartime destruction.

'School' has, for as long as it has served its purpose, been the attractively plain *School* and functional name given to the Monastic Dormitory which was the subject of a Chapter Order in 1599:

> It is decreed by Mr Deane and the Prebendaries present, that in respect that the now Schole howse is to low and to litle to conteyne the number of Schollers, that the old Dorter, of late yeares begun to be made a larger Schole, shalbe, with all convenient spede, turned to that good use, for the benefyt of the Schollers, by such charitable contributions as may be gathered for the fynishing therof.

The muddled and disappointing impression the space now makes in comparison with the primitive magnificence of the old prints, photographs and memories, has to be pieced out with a blend of knowledge and imagination. The Dorter was a late eleventh century building. The voussoirs of alternate tufa and stone on some of the old doorways, and the rounded arches in the south wall provide the best evidence at this level, despite the misleadingly refaced stonework. To visit the Undercroft below, and to see the whole building supported by great oak trees of pillars, removes all doubts. A fire in 1298 destroyed many of the monastic buildings, after which tracery was added to the original Norman windows. This feature is still visible in two blocked windows at each end of the room. Until 1941 the roof was a plain oak hammerbeam of the sixteenth century. Of that time too is the iron bar, rescued from the debris of war and put back in place in 1946 when the

117

A niche of the former St Dunstan's Chapel, on the east side of the Undercroft of the monastic dormitory. The relic now keeps unlikely company in an extension of the gymnasium.

room was still roofless. This was the curtain bar for the separation of Upper from Under School, over which the pancake is tossed for the Shrove Tuesday Greaze. Extensive building work in the Schoolroom in 1659 included a 'neech', which may have been the first 'Shell', a shallow recess in the form of an arc at the north end of the room. It may have been for the Electors, or for those elected to make their valedictory orations from. The narrow space behind it, between School and the Abbey Library have been at various times part of a Minor Canon's house, the living quarters of the Abbey Librarian, and the Rod room, where first boys themselves, and later servants, put together birch rods for use in School. Reconstruction in 1868 merged the space with the rest of the School. In that same reconstruction a piece of twisted column from the Confessor's shrine was found among the rubble filling in the old Norman windows at the south end. A similar piece was found in 1905 when the foundations for the Science Building were being dug on the site of the Abbey's kitchen garden. Both pieces are now back in place on the shrine.

For much of its time, School was a bleak and ruinous place. The windows were always kept broken; there were no fires, and the first heating was by water pipes in 1837. In 1814 the stone side walls were in a state of collapse, and were rebuilt in brick while the roof was precariously supported: so the total ruin of 1941 was somehow a natural progression. After the war, replacement of the hammerbeam roof was contemplated, but the additional cost (about £45,000 in 1950) compelled the Governors to settle for something simpler. The past was recalled in other ways: by the replacement of coats of arms of Old Westminsters originally set up by Rutherford in 1889, and by the reinstatement of an odd mechanical shell nearly a hundred years after the original had been swept away, which rises ponderously at the press of a button to reveal a stage with an inhibiting proscenium arch, its shape dictated by the 'Mark II' shell. If anyone could have anticipated the growth of the School in the years since reconstruction, the room would have been opened out to its fullest dimensions. When the whole School gathers for Latin Prayers, a right granted by the Act of Uniformity of 1662 to Oxford, Cambridge, Convocation, Westminster, Winchester and Eton, a proportion of absenteeism is required for the pupils to fit in; when candidates gather for internal examinations, the desks have to be placed in sociable relationship.

Gymnasium

In a deep well in the angle between the Dormitory and the Chapter House lurks the Gymnasium, built for the School in 1861 on the site of the monks' cemetery. Though it appears to be of no interest, but for a comic curve in a straight wall to avoid a flying buttress, its west wall is the original outer wall of the Dorter, and beneath its paint and plaster are massive square blocks of Norman masonry. The ante-chamber is much older than the main gymnasium, and was the fourteenth century Chapel of St Dunstan. A battered but delicately carved niche in its south wall is hidden behind weightlifting equipment and vaulting horses.

Rere-Dorter

The best preserved antiquity lies deeper still. At right angles to the Dorter at the south end was the Rere-Dorter, which inconveniently stood athwart the entrance to the main cloister, which became, for obvious reasons, the Dark Cloister. After the Dissolution the Rere-Dorter was promptly demolished. But its Undercroft remains, below ground level. For the Benedictines it served both as a monks' prison, and as a kitchen; later it was divided into two wine cellars, one for Ashburnham, the other for the Prebendal House built by Busby in the Little Cloister. Next it was a storeroom for the Latin Play scenery, and then an airless rabbit warren of sound-proofed cells for music lessons. Now it is again its elemental self, a barrel vault with the marks of the eleventh century shuttering still discernible in the mortar, a stone arch like a rainbow, and a narrow, possibly Saxon window obviously older than the vault which swallows it up.

The Busby Library, known to Busby and his successors as the Museum, stands at the south end of School, in the angle between that building and the houses in Little Cloister. Dean Williams first set aside for the School a library room on the site, but it was confiscated by the Chapter when Williams was sent to the Tower in 1637. The Parliamentary Committee restored it to the School when it abolished Chapters. Bricklayers' and carpenters' accounts suggest that Busby rebuilt it between 1657 and 1659, though the original ceiling, with its shallow domes garlanded with plasterwork, must have been added later, almost certainly in 1680 or 1681, when Busby built for himself an adjacent Prebendal house with almost identical designs on its ceilings. Robert Hooke, a former pupil, may have assisted Busby at this stage of the work; they were certainly in close contact at this period. On his death, Busby divided his books between the Museum, the parish of Willen, in Northamptonshire, and parishes in Wells, where he was a prebendary. His catalogue of his best books, written in his own hand in the last year of his life, identifies about four hundred books which remain in the Library, among them books given by Mildred, Lady Burghley and signed by Roger Ascham, books from Wynkin de Worde, Caxton's successor at the presses in the precinct, and first editions of Descartes' *Discours de la Methode*, *Lycidas*, and *Paradise Lost*, still in the School's possession.

Busby Library

The prologue to the Latin Play in 1726 laments the ruinous condition of the old Dormitory. The Scholars had been expecting new premises for fifteen years. Sir Edward Hannes, Queen Anne's oculist, who died in 1711 left £1000 in his will to provide a new home for them. Wren was consulted, and reported that the sum was insufficient. Atterbury revived the project at the accession of George I, and raised over £3000 more, largely from the King, the Prince of Wales and Parliament. Financial delays then yielded to delays caused by indecision and division in the Chapter, which in turn found its way as a legal issue to the House of Lords. In a very wandering hand, the eighty-eight year old Wren put his signature in 1719 to an opinion in favour of the site in 'the College Common Orchard or garden', but Burlington had to wait until 1722 to lay his foundation stone, the Scholars until October 1729 for the windows of the Old Dormitory to be finally boarded up. The seats and scenes for the Play were constructed in the new building at the end of November.

College Dormitory

Burlington's Dormitory, one of the earliest buildings in London to use Bath stone, drew its inspiration partly from Palladio's cloister at San Giorgio Maggiore, in Venice, and partly from Inigo Jones's piazzas in Covent Garden. Its dimensions closely matched those of the Granary, and its ground floor open piazza echoed the stabling for carts and wagons in the old building, though with statues in niches replacing the hay racks. Soon the windows were broken, and

the rats moved in, and the new Dormitory rapidly came to resemble the old. In two respects at least, though, it was superior: it was not tumbling down around the Scholars, and at its three great fireplaces, more Seniors could warm themselves to the exclusion of fewer Juniors. The last task of the day of these same Juniors until well into the next century was to tip water the length of the floor on winter nights so that an ice slide would be there for the next morning's sport.

The clearance of Little Dean's Yard, completed in the 1780s, was the stimulus for the construction of a terrace of three houses by Robert Furze Brettingham in 1790, two of which remain, fortunate in possessing unsurpassed views of the Abbey. They replaced a much decayed great house called Vaughans, an early Tudor mansion with a courtyard, a 'great staircase in the great turret' and a garden bounded by the millstream, with open country beyond. Vaughans was desirable enough to be coveted by Protector Somerset in 1549, and the Chapter resisted with the argument that it had been assigned as a Prebendal house, but as soon as Somerset had been fobbed off with the gift of the stone of the Refectory to build Somerset House, it reverted to a private residence and was leased to the Bishop of Norwich in 1552. In 1620 it was inherited by Dudley Carleton, Viscount Dorchester, and became known for a time as Dorchester House after he remodelled it. Robert Freind, Head Master (1711–33), turned it into two 'very airy' boarding houses, to receive 'about 80 sons of the Nobility and Gentry', and

Above left. A modern view of the remaining houses of Brettingham's terrace of 1790, number 2 and 3, Little Dean's Yard.

Above right. A detail of the Elizabethan fireplace of 1596 in Ashburnham House.

Left. The front door of 3 Little Dean's Yard, the home of the Master of the Queen's Scholars, showing the sedan chair steps and fanlight which were part of Robert Furze Brettingham's design of 1790.

installed 'Dames' to look after them. One of these was Dame Grant, who occupied part of this house from 1751 to 1790. In 1790 the lease of the new central house was assigned to her son, Rev. Richard Grant, and the Grant family continued to run the house until 1847, when Liddell turned out a fearsome Dame known as 'Mother Jones' or 'the Black Serjeant'. The eastern wing of the old house may have been rebuilt rather than replaced. The tablet over the front door of 3 Little Dean's Yard, the house of the Master of the Scholars, suggests as much in the word 'Restauravit', and in the basement of this house there is a great kitchen fireplace that belongs to an earlier century. Brettingham himself and his family held the lease of the right-hand house, 1 Little Dean's Yard, until about 1840, though it was in use as a boarding house from its early days. The plainness of Brettingham's terrace was so unpleasing to the taste of the late Victorians that they had no qualms about demolishing this house in 1896, and replacing it by a multicoloured brick fantasy, with classical motifs, by T. G. Jackson. Its name, Rigauds, derives from a housemaster, Stephen George Rigaud, who spent only four years in the house (1846–50), for his ambitions led him to the Bishopric of Antigua via the headmastership of Ipswich. Another name from the past which survived beyond reasonable expectations was 'Chiswicks', by which the sick rooms in College and the other two houses on the terrace were originally known. Chiswick as a place of refuge in times of sickness was rarely, if ever, used by the school after 1700, but only as the Head Master's country residence, and the last man to use it had been Markham, in the 1760s. So the appearance of the name after 1790 suggests a continuity of reference throughout the eighteenth century. The name survives in the 1980s only in Grants, and there it no longer even refers to sick rooms. Another feature of all three houses, as early prints show, was matching sets of sedan chair steps. Grants and Rigauds lost theirs in 1885 and 1896, perhaps prematurely, since a sedan chair was still in use in the Cloisters in 1897, when Miss Agatha Thynne was carried home after her presentation at Court.

Ashburnham House
Ashburnham House, over which the Abbey and the School went to war in 1881, has a rich and complex history; of all the buildings it is the nub and epitome of the School's long life. The remains of two earlier houses are embedded in it: the Prior's House, a large rambling but narrow building which grew over four centuries between 1100 and 1500. The original north wall of this house is now the spine of the present house, which runs on east through cellars and boiler room as far as the Dark Cloister. Its stone west gable is clearly visible outside; its kitchen is now the inner room of the School Store, and fifteenth century windows remain in the wall of the principal ground floor room. For the ten years in which Westminster had a bishop (1540–50), this house became the Deanery. It was still known as the Dean's House when it was leased in 1599 to Sir John Fortescue, Chancellor of Elizabeth's Exchequer. Of his rebuilt house, only the ground floor fireplace survives. In 1662, a new lease was assigned to William Ashburnham, Cofferer of the Household, companion of Charles II in Paris during the Commonwealth, and friend of Pepys. Surprisingly for so celebrated a house, there is no evidence which puts either its architect or its date beyond question. Opinion has shifted from Inigo Jones and the 1630s to William Samwell and the

1660s, partly on the evidence of the use of domes and of the plasterwork. For three generations only did the Ashburnhams enjoy their pleasance, riding in from their country estate near Rye, it is said, on their own land all the way. The last Ashburnham to live there was John, First Earl, married to Lady Mary Butler, 'greatest favourite' of Swift. In 1730 it was leased to the Crown as the repository for the King's and Cottonian Libraries, on the grounds that it was safe from fire. Dr Bentley, Master of Trinity and curator of the collection, moved in with it, but in the following year when fire broke out from a smouldering chimney beam, he fled from the house in his nightgown and great wig, though clutching the Alexandrian Codex. The copies of Magna Carta and the Manuscript of Beowulf in the British Museum still bear the singe marks from this fire. The old Granary, though tumbledown, found a last use in housing the surviving volumes gathered up in the next few days from the neighbourhood.

The Dean and Chapter enquired about the purchase of Lord Ashburnham's house in 1736. The clearance of buildings on the north side of the Abbey, in St Margaret's Churchyard, had lost them two prebendal houses, and they were obviously eager to regain what had once been the Deanery. Purchase was completed in 1739, for £500, and it was adapted to form two residences, however

The plaster work of the Drawing Room of Ashburnham House 1662–65. The original hollow dome of this ceiling was lost when a top storey was added to the house while it was a Chapter residence in the nineteenth century.

A fire in 1730 damaged Ashburnham House and the Cottonian Library then housed there. The reconstruction produced a riot of plaster ornament (*above left*) reminiscent of a wedding cake.

A turn in the grand staircase of Ashburnham House by William Samwell 1662–65, a detail showing the balance of ornament and simplicity in the design (*above right*).

The carved door frame in Ashburnham Drawing Room, 1662–65.

inconvenient. Some of this inconvenience was relieved when an extra storey was added in the nineteenth century, but at the cost of destroying the dome in the first floor drawing room. Lord John Thynne, as canon and sub-dean, lived in each of these houses in turn for a total of forty-four years, so this reluctance even to think of their passing to the school was entirely natural. The School took possession of Ashburnham in 1882, and though there were regrettable losses, of the little stone gatehouse in front, and the summer house in the garden, the threatened demolition of the entire place was averted. Initially a new day boy house, called Ashburnham, was installed on the ground floor, and the fine rooms of the first floor became a library in commemoration of Scott's headmastership, as they still remain. Of these rooms, J. M. W. Halley wrote in the *Architectural Review* in 1910, 'there are more gorgeous rooms in the world . . . but none more peaceful, none more full of sweetness and light, than these seventeenth century rooms of which the great drawing room at Ashburnham house is the finest'. So far from its being a violation of them, as some have suggested, to make the boys and girls of the School their primary residents, it is the means of admitting more people to that sweetness and light than was ever possible in the past, and at an age when such qualities are likely to remain with them for a lifetime.

The small garden between Ashburnham House and the Cloisters shares in the house's history. It was the site of the monastic Refectory; its north and east walls were once the internal walls of that refectory; beneath the grass are the remains of

Two views of Ashburnham Drawing Room, 1986 (*above*) and c. 1910 (*below*).

its fourteenth century tiled floor, and angel corbels like those in College Hall, but now weathered beyond identification, support an imaginary roof. On the north wall, chunky Norman arcading at the lower level is disdained by the more delicate outlines of the fourteenth century blocked windows high in the wall beneath the corbels. In the twelfth and thirteenth centuries, the Commons met both in the Chapter House and the Refectory. Here in 1162 the announcement was made of Thomas à Becket's election as Archbishop of Canterbury, and here later Edward II's barons met to conspire against Piers Gaveston. The Refectory was an early victim of the Dissolution. In 1544 one Guy Gasker was instructed 'forthwith in all haste for the avoiding of further inconveniens take down the frater house'. The air of decayed quiet which now presides is preferable to its becoming a mason's yard, which was proposed after the School took possession. Then the ghost of the monk appointed to read the scriptures at meal times would have been heard by no-one.

Turle's House   Adjacent to Ashburnham House, on the east side, was the house known in the nineteenth century as Turle's House, after Turle, the Abbey organist, who lived in it from 1841 till his death in 1882. This was a rambling medieval and Tudor house, with picturesque dormers, chimneys and roofs, to which roof-climbing boys were much attached. Among its internal eccentricities was a room with no natural light, which was lit by a kind of diagonal well shaft that had to pass through a room nearer the sun. In the seventeenth century it probably supplied bedroom accommodation, otherwise inexplicably absent from Ashburnham itself, and, together with that house, it became a prebendal residence in 1739. Dr Taylor, Johnson's friend, lived here from 1751 to 1760, and was caused to get up to go at once to comfort him when Johnson's letter announcing the death of his wife arrived at three o'clock one morning. When the School acquired Turle's in 1882 on the organist's death, it was thought inconvenient for school use and unworthy of preservation, so it was demolished in 1883. During its demolition, one of the original Norman windows of the Dormitory with its T-shaped decorated capitals intact, was discovered buried deep in the wall it shared with the School. It remains, but still buried deep beneath the floor of one of the classrooms in the unlovely block built by Pearson on the site of a house which, if it had remained, would by now be one of the few domestic survivals of Tudor London.

18 Dean's Yard   18 Dean's Yard, originally the Monk Bailiff's house, alternated between private and prebendal residence between the Dissolution and 1883, when it too came to the School via the Public Schools Act, in what the Dean and Chapter must have felt was the biggest legalised robbery since 1540. The Public Schools Commission had been preoccupied with the circulation of air as a guarantor of health, and had recommended that this house be pulled down, in whole or in part, to admit west winds to Little Dean's Yard. The Chapter promptly enlarged the house, and gave a fresh lease to a new tenant. From 1885 until 1939, it housed 'Home-Boarders', a day house whose name cleverly disguised the School's reluctance to admit the drift towards day pupils.

17 Dean's Yard   17 Dean's Yard, acquired for the School in the 1930s, had been built in 1808, a Regency reconstruction of an earlier monastic building. It was a prebendal house from its first days, linked particularly with St Margaret's Church. The last clerical

Turle's house, in the north-east corner of Little Dean's Yard, in 1881. The year before, the death of James Turle, the abbey organist, gave the School the option of purchase under the terms of the Public Schools Act of 1868. This Elizabethan fantasy of chimneys and gables was a tempting playground for roof climbers. It was demolished in 1883 to make way for the present classroom block.

resident was Canon Carnegie, whose wife, the widow of Joseph Chamberlain, was the grande-dame of the precincts. The Carnegies kept a carriage which they regularly used for local evening parties. The first floor drawing room was rescued from use as a biology laboratory when it became the Head Master's house in 1950, though he has to share his front door with nearly one hundred full and part-time staff who crowd for tea, biscuits and relief from their pupils into two ground floor rooms.

Barton Street

Barton Street, where the School owns a number of Georgian houses, began life as a building speculation by Barton Booth, the Old Westminster actor, who took a lease on the Ostery garden and began the expansion of Westminster beyond the Mill Stream, marked by and hidden under the line of Great College Street, just beyond the precinct wall. Barton Street, and Cowley Street, at right angles to it, were built between 1722 and 1725. Though the dainty streets have lost their public house at the corner, and their nineteenth century reputation for squalor, they have gained Westminster's girl boarders, and the frequent invasion of film companies.

Vincent Square

Vincent Square, some five minutes walk from the School to the south west, past the arid environment of the Department of that name, is the last ten acres of the former Tothill Fields. From at least the time of Henry III, the fields were in use as a 'placee' (from the Latin plateae), or a tournament ground, a place for fighting and the settlement of wagers. It was also the site of the great Tothill Fair, revenue from which Henry III secured to help finance the building of the Abbey. The openness of the Fields, with their many ditches and ponds, was a particular lure for Westminster boys, and provided them with a great variety of physical challenges and sporting distractions, from shooting and skating to ditch-leaping and donkey racing, in addition to some of the earliest cricket matches on record. The prerogatives of Westminsters are still recorded in some of the Pimlico place names: King's Scholars Passage, Pond and Pumping Station, King's Scholar Sewer. As building encroachment intensified at the beginning of the nineteenth century, William Vincent, Head Master turned Dean, marked off ten acres with a plough in 1810, and set it aside for the exclusive use of the School by surrounding it with a ditch or trench to keep off carts and carriages. The total cost of this far-sighted annexation was £3. 1s. This use was confirmed by the Public Schools Act, though after the Second World War the school had to fight doggedly to resist its acquisition by city hall as an amenity for the general public and a playground for the local children. Additional strands of barbed wire, impulsively put up a few years ago without planning permission, were ordered to be taken down, so the more daring and athletic of the local residents still have a sporting chance.

9

SELECTED LIST OF OLD WESTMINSTERS

ROBERT BEAUMONT 1527–1567. Master of Trinity and Vice-Chancellor of Cambridge. Calvinist divine.

EDWARD GRANT 1544?–1601. Head Master. Noted scholar, friend of Roger Ascham.

WILLIAM MORGAN 1547?–1604. Bishop of Llandaff and St Asaph; translator of Bible into Welsh.

RICHARD EDES 1552?–1604. Chaplain to Elizabeth and James I. Translator of the Bible.

RICHARD HAKLUYT 1553–1616. Geographer and compiler of travels.

WILLIAM GOODWIN 1555?–1620. Dean of Christ Church and Vice-Chancellor. Preacher who caused the whole city of Oxford to 'shed fountains of tears' in funeral sermon for Prince Henry, 1612.

WILLIAM GAGER 1555?–1622. Latin dramatist and poet.

LEONARD HUTTEN 1555?–1632. Latin poet; translator of the Bible; antiquary.

JOHN KING 1557?–1621. Bishop of London 'King of Preachers' (James I). Last bishop to burn a heretic. (artist unknown)

THOMAS RAVIS 1560?–1609. Bishop of Gloucester; translator of the Bible.

RICHARD NEILE 1561–1640. Archbishop of York.

WILLIAM ALABASTER 1567–1640. Poet and dramatist.

WILLIAM DAKINS 1569?–1607. Professor of Divinity at Gresham College. Translator of the Bible.

ROBERT COTTON 1570–1631. Collector: Cottonian Library.

RICHARD IRELAND 1571–1636? Head Master.

BEN JONSON. 1573–1637. Poet and dramatist. (after Van Blijenberch)

DUDLEY CARLETON, VISCOUNT DORCHESTER 1573–1632. Diplomat.

JOHN BOWLE 1576?–1637. Bishop of Rochester.

ARTHUR DEE 1580?–1651. Hermetic philosopher. Friend of Sir Thomas Browne. Physician to the Tsar.

EDMUND GUNTER 1581–1621. Mathematician and astronomer. Discovered variation of magnetic needle.

RICHARD CORBET 1582–1635. Bishop of Oxford and Norwich. Poet and friend of Ben Jonson.

GODFREY GOODMAN 1583–1666. Bishop of Gloucester. Involved in controversy. Palace sacked; imprisoned in Tower. Died in poverty. A lifelong secret Catholic.

RICHARD LANE 1584–1650. Counsel for Strafford. Lord Keeper of the Great Seal 1645; followed Charles II into exile.

THOMAS HOWARD, 2nd Earl of Arundel 1586–1646. Earl Marshal; Lord Steward of the Household; Lord High Steward at Stafford's trial. Art collector. Settled and died at Padua.

WILLIAM BEALE 1588?–1651. Royalist divine. Master of Jesus and St Johns, Vice-Chancellor of Cambridge. Imprisoned in Tower. Died in Madrid.

BRIAN DUPPA 1588–1662. Bishop of Winchester. Lord High Almoner.

GILES FLETCHER 1588?–1623. Poet and Greek scholar.

HENRY KING 1592–1669. Bishop of Chichester. Friend of Ben Jonson and John Donne. Poet; celebrated preacher.

CHARLES CHAUNCY 1592–1672. President of Harvard 1654–72.

GEORGE HERBERT 1593–1633. Poet. Public Orator, Cambridge 1619–27. (artist unknown)

ROBERT CREIGHTON 1593–1672. Bishop of Bath and Wells.

LAMBERT OSBALDSTON 1594?–1659. Head Master.

GEORGE MORLEY 1597–1684. Chaplain to King in Civil War; in exile with Charles II. Bishop of Worcester and Winchester after the Restoration. Preacher of Coronation Sermon 1661.

ARTHUR HESILRIGGE 1600?–1661. Puritan. Introduced Bill of Attainder against Strafford. Leader of Independents in Parliament. Opposed Cromwell after dissolution of Long Parliament. Died a prisoner in the Tower.

JOHN PRICE 1600–1676? Greek scholar. Professor of Greek at University of Pisa. Served Grand Duke Ferdinand II in Florence and Cardinal Barberini in Rome.

WILLIAM STRODE 1602–1645. Poet and dramatist.

THOMAS LOCKEY 1602–1679. Classical scholar; collector of books, pictures and coins; Bodley's Librarian.

JOHN MARSHAM 1602–1685. The first serious English scholar of Egyptian antiquities.

JOHN GLYNNE 1603–1666. Chief Justice under Cromwell. King's Serjeant 1660.

JOHN DONNE 1604–1663. Son of the poet; editor of his father's poems.

JASPER MAYNE 1604–1672. 'A quaint preacher and a noted poet'. Playwright; translator of Lucian, Chaplain to Charles II.

THOMAS RANDOLPH 1605–1635. Close friend of Ben Jonson; Latin and English poet, playwright.

JAMES DUPORT 1606–1679. Greek scholar; translator of Prayer Book into Greek.

RICHARD BUSBY 1606–1695. Head Master.

WILLIAM CARTWRIGHT 1611–1643. Poet and dramatist. Member of King's War Council.

ROBERT WARING 1614–1658. Latin and English poet. Camden Professor of Ancient History.

THOMAS SCOT 1615?–60. Regicide. Member of the five Councils of State during the Commonwealth. Manager of home and foreign intelligence. Secretary of State 1660. Fled to Flanders, surrendered to the King's resident in Brussels. Hanged at Charing Cross, October 1660.

HENRY VANE 1613–1662. Became a puritan at school. Went to New England for freedom of worship; Governor of Massachusetts at 23. Parliamentarian during the Commonwealth. Failed to reconcile the army and Parliament, and expelled from the House 1660. Executed on Tower Hill for High Treason 1662. (*after Miereveldt*)

ROGER L'ESTRANGE 1616–1704. Ardent royalist. Escaped from death sentence at Newgate 1648. Surveyor of the Press 1663. Burnt in effigy by London mob when he tried to disprove the existence of a popish plot. Often in prison after 1688. Pamphleteer and author.

HENRY BENNET, Earl of Arlington 1618?–1685. Member of the Cabal.

ABRAHAM COWLEY 1618–1667. Poet, diplomat, royalist spy.

JAMES QUIN 1621–1659. Ejected from studentship at Christ Church for non-submission, but restored to it by Cromwell, who was charmed by his singing voice. Insane from 1651 until his death.

HENEAGE FINCH, 1st Earl of Norttingham 1621–1682. Lord Chancellor. Lord High Steward. 'Amri' in Absalom and Achitophel.

EDMUND GODFREY 1621–1678. Justice. Zealous Protestant. Found dead in a ditch on Primrose Hill. Linked with the Titus Oates plot.

JOHN DOLBEN, F.R.S. 1625–1686. Dean of Westminister. Archbishop of York.

JOHN BABER 1625–1704. Physician to Charles II.

WALTER POPE 1627?–1714. Succeeded Wren as Professor of Astronomy at Gresham College. Founder member of Royal Society 1663.

THOMAS MILLINGTON 1628–1704. Professor of Natural Philosophy at Oxford. Physician to William and Anne. Discoverer of sexuality in plants.

NICHOLAS HOOKES 1628–1712. Poet.

JAMES HEATH 1629–1664. Royalist historian.

NATHANIEL HODGES 1629–1688. City physician during Great Plague.

JOHN DRYDEN 1631–1700. Poet and dramatist. Poet Laureate.

PHILIP HENRY 1631–1696. Favourite pupil of Busby. Non-conformist preacher. Imprisoned until passing of Act of Toleration.

HENRY STUBBE 1632–1676. Noted Latin and Greek scholar, but a thorn in the flesh of authority. Whipped for abusing the Censor at Christ Church; ejected from Oxford for writing 'a pestilent book' against the clergy and the universities. Imprisoned for denouncing James's marriage with Mary of Modena. Friend of Hobbes.

RICHARD LOWER 1632–1691. Physician to Charles II. Experimental physiologist and anatomist. First to transfuse blood from one animal to another.

JOHN LOCKE 1632–1704. Philosopher.
(*Brounower* c. 1685)

CHRISTOPHER WREN 1632–1723. Original fellow of Royal Society. Professor of Astronomy at Gresham College and Oxford. Architect. (*Kneller* 1711).

ROBERT SAWYER 1633–1692. Speaker of the Commons. Attorney General 1681–7; conducted Rye House Plot prosecutions, and appeared against Titus Oates. Expelled from the Commons 1690.

JOSEPH WILLIAMSON 1633–1701. Keeper of the King's Whitehall Library; editor of the London Gazette; Secretary of State and Commissioner of the Admiralty.

FRANCIS VERNON, F.R.S. 1634?–1677. Traveller. Murdered by Arabs near Isfahan during a quarrel about a penknife.

ROBERT SOUTH 1634–1716. Chaplain to Charles II.

THOMAS GALE 1635–1702. Dean of York. Antiquary and collector.

ROBERT HOOKE 1635–1703. Inventor, mechanic, architect, astronomer. Spiral spring to regulate watches, principle of the arch. Author of *Micrographia*.

CHARLES SACKVILLE, F.R.S. 6th Earl of Dorset 1638–1706. Courtier and wit. Lord Chamberlain to the Household 1689–97.

RALPH MONTAGU, 1st Duke 1638–1709. Diplomat. Supporter of Monmouth. Promoter in the Lords of the 1688 Revolution.

THOMAS KNIPE 1639–1711. Head Master.

GEORGE HOOPER 1640–1727. Bishop of Bath and Wells. 'The best scholar, the finest gentleman, and will make the completest bishop that ever was educated at Westminster School' (Busby).

LEONARD PLUKENET 1642–1706. Superintendant of Royal Gardens, Hampton Court. Queen's Botanist.

ROBERT UVEDALE 1642–1722. Snatcher of the Majesty Scutcheon from Cromwell's bier. Skilled cultivator of exotic plants, and owner of one of the first hothouses in England. Wrote a 14 volume Herbarium.

RICHARD SAVAGE, 4th Earl Rivers 1644?–1712. 'Tyburn Dick' – a handsome, unscrupulous rake. The first nobleman to give his allegiance to William of Orange in 1688. General of the Horse.

ROGER ALTHAM 1646?–1714. Regius Professor of Hebrew.

ROBERT ATKYNS 1647–1711. Topographer.

DANIEL BURGESS 1647?–1713. Celebrated non-conformist preacher; meeting house in Lincoln's Inn Fields burnt down by Sacheverell mob 1710.

DANIEL FINCH, 2nd Earl of Nottingham 1647–1730. President of Council. Head of high church party under Anne. Secretary of State.

GEORGE LEGGE, 1st Baron Dartmouth 1648–1691. Admiral and C in C Fleet 1688. Failure to prevent Dutch ships approaching coast led to conspiracy against William III. Died of apoplexy in the Tower.

GEORGE JEFFREYS, 1st Baron 1648–1689. Lord Chief Justice of the Bloody Assize. Lord Chancellor. Died a prisoner in the Tower. (*Claret* c. 1678).

RICHARD GRAHAM, 1st Viscount Preston 1648–1695. Diplomat and Secretary of State under James II. Arrested and sentenced to death for carrying treasonable papers, 1691. Pardoned for implicating others. Translator of Boethius.

HUMPHREY PRIDEAUX 1648–1724. Hebrew scholar. Declined Oxford Professorship of Hebrew 1691. Wrote Life of Mahomet. Dean of Norwich.

ELKANAH SETTLE 1648–1724. Playwright. Involved in literary war with Dryden because of the success of his bombastic pieces. City Laureate 1691. Object of ridicule in *The Dunciad*.

CARR SCROOPE 1649–1680. Versifier; man of fashion.

JONATHAN TRELAWNY 1650–1721. Active opponent of Monmouth's rebellion 1685. Bishop of Bristol. Sent to the Tower in 1688 but acquitted of seditious libel. Took oath to William and Mary, Bishop of Exeter and Winchester thereafter.

JAMES GRAHAM 1650–1730. Confidant of James II, and assisted him in his flight. Outlawed and arrested, but took oaths of loyalty in 1701.

NATHANIEL LEE 1653–1692. Playwright. Collaborator with Dryden. Became insane because of intemperate habits, and confined to Bedlam for 5 years.

RICHARD BLACKMORE 1654–1729. Physician to William III and Anne. Poet, theologian, historian.

CHARLES MORDAUNT, 3rd Earl of Peterborough 1658?–1735. Initiator of the Glorious Revolution; landed with William at Torbay. First Lord of Treasury. Joint commander of Spanish expedition 1705; captured Barcelona. Diplomat. Patron of literature and science.

LAUNCELOT BLACKBURNE 1658–1743. Buccaneer and Archbishop of York. A witty and scandalous divine who 'retained nothing of his first profession except his seraglio'. (Walpole)

NICHOLAS BRADY 1659–1726. Chaplain to William and Mary, and Anne. Co-author of metrical psalms.

WHITE KENNETT 1660–1728. Bishop of Peterborough. Zealous Whig. Founder member of Society for Propagation of Gospel. Antiquary and historian.

CHARLES MONTAGU, Earl of Halifax 1661–1715. Orator and financier. Originator of the Bank of England and the National Debt. First Lord of the Treasury. Friend of Newton; patron of literature; President of the Royal Society.

GEORGE SMALRIDGE 1662–1719. Bishop of Bristol and Lord High Almoner. Friend of Atterbury. Removed on his refusal to sign the declaration against the Pretender 1715.

THOMAS PARKYNS 1662–1741. Magistrate, architect, engineer, collector of stone coffins.

FRANCIS GASTRELL 1662–1725. Bishop of Chester.

GEORGE STEPNEY 1663–1707. Diplomat, poet, friend of Dryden.

FRANCIS ATTERBURY 1663–1732. Dean of Westminster and Bishop of Rochester. Exiled as a Jacobite.

MATTHEW PRIOR 1664–1721. Son of a joiner. Diplomat and poet. Negotiated Treaty of Utrecht. Impeached and imprisoned by Walpole. Buried, by his wish, 'at the feet of Spenser' in the Abbey.

WILLIAM CADOGAN, 1st Earl 1672–1726. Major-General under Marlborough, succeeded him as C in C of the Forces.

WILLIAM SHIPPEN 1673–1743. Tory politician and satirist. Sent to the Tower for drawing attention to George I's ignorance of England in 1718. A courageous and incorruptible man, and the founder of constitutional opposition in the Commons.

JAMES BRYDGES, 1st Duke of Chandos 1673–1744. Builder of Canons and patron of Handel.

SAMUEL D'OYLY 1680?–1748. Army Chaplain in Flanders 'too corpulent for any horse to carry him'.

RICHARD FREWIN 1680?–1761. Professor of Chemistry and Ancient History. Noted physician. Left his house (Frewin Hall) to Reg. Prof. of Medicine.

BARTON BOOTH 1681–1733. Actor.

BROWNE WILLIS 1682–1760. Antiquary.

ROBERT JOHNSON 1682–1735. Governor of South Carolina.

JOHN PERCEVAL, 1st Earl of Egmont 1683–1748. First resident of the Province of Georgia, and superintended its colonisation.

JOHN NICOL 1683–1765. Head Master.

EDWARD BIRD 1684?–1719. Transferred to Eton and subsequently hanged at Tyburn for murdering a waiter.

DANIEL PULTENEY 1684–1731. Lord of the Admiralty. Clerk of the Council in Ireland. Fierce opponent of Walpole, failure to overthrow whom led to his excessive drinking and death.

EDWARD VERNON 1684–1757. Admiral of the White. 'Old Grog' to the Navy. Commander of West Indies expedition 1739–42.

WILLIAM PULTENEY, Earl of Bath 1684–1764. Secretary at War 1714–17. Quarrelled with Walpole and dismissed 1725; ally of Bolingbroke. Duelled with Lord Hervey in Green Park 1731. Head of the Ministry for 2 days in 1746.

LIONEL SACKVILLE, 1st Duke of Dorset 1688–1765. Lord-Lieutenant of Ireland. Lord President of the Council. Lord Warden of the Cinque Ports.

AARON HILL 1685–1750. Theatre Manager; playwright and pamphleteer. First professional theatre critic.

JOHN HEYLYN 1686?–1759. Chaplain to George II: 'the Mystic Doctor'.

HENRY BOYLE, 1st Earl of Shannon 1687?–1764. Whig speaker of Irish House of Commons: 'the King of the Irish Commons'.

EDWARD HARLEY, 2nd Earl of Oxford 1689–1741. Friend of Pope and Swift. Collector of books and manuscripts, the basis of the Harleian Collection in the British Museum.

JOHN CARTERET, 2nd Earl Granville 1690–1763. Lord Lieutenant of Ireland. Lord President of the Council. Friend of Swift.
(Studio of Hoare c. 1750).

THOMAS PELHAM-HOLLES, Duke of Newcastle 1693–1768. First Lord of Treasury 1754–6; 1757–62. Chancellor of Cambridge.

JOHN HERVEY, Baron Hervey of Ickworth 1696–1743. Intimate of Queen Caroline and Walpole. Satirised by Pope as 'Sporus' and 'Lord Fanny'.

HENRY PELHAM 1696–1754. Supporter of Walpole, First Lord of the Treasury and Chancellor of the Exchequer 1743–54.

JOHN DYER 1700–1757. Poet.

THOMAS NEWTON 1703–1782. Bishop of Bristol; patron of Garrick.

BEAUPRE BELL 1704?–1741. Collector; antiquary; numismatist. 'One of the first wits of this country'. (Johnson)

THOMAS BEDFORD 1705–1773. Prominent non-juring minister.

WILLIAM MURRAY, 1st Earl of Mansfield 1705–1793. 'The father of modern toryism' – (Macaulay). Chief Justice for 32 years. Pillar of Newcastle's administrations. Outstanding orator. House sacked and burned in the Gordon Riots, 1780. Close friend of Pope.

JOHN BOYLE 1707–1762. Earl of Cork and Orrery. Man of letters. Friend of Pope, Swift, and Johnson.

CHARLES WESLEY 1707–1788. Methodist preacher and writer of over 6000 hymns.

RICHARD ROBINSON, 1st Baron Rokeby 1708?–1794. Archbishop of Armagh and Primate of Ireland. Provided funds for Canterbury Quad at Christ Church. Left a bequest to establish a university in Ulster.

WILLIAM BECKFORD, of Fonthill Abbey 1709–1770. Whig supporter of John Wilkes. Lord Mayor of London.

JOHN WILMOT 1709–1792. Lord Chief Justice of the Common Pleas. Three times refused Lord Chancellorship.

WILLIAM BULL 1710–1791. Speaker of S. Carolina Assembly; Lieutenant Governor and acting Governor of S. Carolina between 1759 and 1775.

STEPHEN DEMAINBRAY 1710–1782. Experimental philosopher and astronomer. Discovered influence of electricity on plant growth.

CHARLES SACKVILLE, 2nd Duke of Dorset 1711–1769. Early cricket enthusiast. Lord of the Treasury. Extravagant man of fashion and patron of opera.

ROBERT HAY DRUMMOND 1711–1776. Archbishop of York.

JOHN CLELAND 1711?–1789. Novelist. Author of *Fanny Hill*.

EDWARD WORTLEY MONTAGU 1713–1776. Dissolute but gifted eccentric. Accomplished Arabist, lived as a Mahometan. Polygamist; gambler. First Englishman to be innoculated against smallpox. Died swallowing a fishbone at Padua.

FRANCIS BERNARD 1713–1779. Governor of Massachusetts Bay and New Jersey.

SIMON HARCOURT, 1st Earl 1714–1777. Ambassador, Lord Lieutenant of Ireland. Drowned trying to extricate his dog from a well.

JAMES WALDEGRAVE, 2nd Earl 1715–1763. First Lord of the Treasury. Premier for five days in 1757.

JAMES HUTTON 1715–1795. Founder of the Moravian Church in England.

GEORGE GERMAIN, 1st Viscount Sackville 1716–1785. Soldier, statesman. Court-martialled and dismissed after Minden, 1759.

PHILIP THICKNESSE 1719–1792. Patron of Gainsborough.

WILLIAM MARKHAM 1719–1807. Head Master. Archbishop of York. Friend of Burke and Hastings.

LAURENCE SHIRLEY, 4th Earl Ferrers 1720–1760. Hanged at Tyburn for shooting his steward, after a trial by his peers in Westminster Hall.

GRANVILLE LEVESON GOWER, 1st Marquis of Stafford 1721–1803. President of the Council.

THOMAS GAGE 1721–1787. General. C in C North America. Governor of Massachusetts 1774.

THOMAS SHERIDAN 1722–1788. Actor-manager and rival of Garrick. Friend of Johnson. Father of R. B. Sheridan.

WILLIAM BYRON, 5th Baron 1722–1798. 'The wicked Lord Byron'. Killed his cousin in a duel; exempted from punishment by his privilege as a peer.

JOHN BURGOYNE 1723–1792. 'Gentleman Johnny'. Lieutenant-General. Dramatist. Surrendered British Army at Saratoga. (*after Ramsay* 1756).

JOHN BYRON 1723–1786. Navigator. Voyage round world in Dolphin 1764–6. Grandfather of the poet.

GEORGE HOWE, 3rd Viscount 1724–1758. Brigadier-General in N. America. Killed in skirmish with French near Ticonderoga.

AUGUSTUS HERVEY, 3rd Earl of Bristol 1724–1779. Vice-Admiral. Served under Byng, Hawke and Keppel. C in C Mediterranean. Lord of the Admiralty.

AUGUSTUS KEPPEL, 1st Viscount 1725–1786. Admiral. C in C Grand Fleet 1778.

MARTIN MADAN 1725–1790. Converted by Wesley's preaching. Travelled the country as Calvinistic Methodist; advocated polygamy, raised a storm of indignation, and retired to the country.

WALTER SHIRLEY 1725–1786. Prominent Calvinistic Methodist and hymn writer. Friend of the Wesleys and Whitfield.

ROBERT MONCKTON 1725–1782. 2nd i/c to Wolfe at Quebec; Governor of New York 1761.

WEST DIGGES 1726–1788. Comic actor.

RICHARD, EARL HOWE 1726–1799. Admiral of the Fleet. Relieved Gibraltar 1784; victory over French 1794; pacified mutineers at Portsmouth 1797. (*Singleton* 1799).

DAVID ROSS 1728–1790. Actor and theatre manager. Presented the first play legally performed in Scotland, at Edinburgh in 1767. Close friend of Boswell.

EDWARD DELAVAL F.R.S. 1729–1814. Physicist.

GEORGE MONSON 1730–1776. Member of Supreme Council of Bengal; opposed Warren Hastings.

CLAYTON CRACHERODE 1730–1799. Collector. Benefactor of British Museum.

CHARLES WATSON-WENTWORTH, 2nd Marquis of Rockingham 1730–1782. Whig statesman. First Lord of the Treasury 1765–6; dismissed by George III for repealing the Stamp Act. Leader of opposition in the Lords 1767–81. In favour of American independence. Second ministry in 1782: curtailed power of Crown. (*Studio of Reynolds*)

FREDERICK HERVEY, 4th Earl of Bristol 1730–1803. Bishop of Derry. Traveller and eccentric. Liberal divine: advocate of relaxation of laws against Catholics.

WILLIAM HAMILTON 1730–1803. Collector of Greek vases and antiquities. British envoy at Naples. Husband of Emma Hamilton.

THOMAS KING 1730–1805. Actor and theatre manager. Original Sir Peter Teazle in *School for Scandal* 1777, and Puff in *The Critic*, 1779. Ruined himself by gambling. Married a hornpipe dancer.

CHARLES CHURCHILL 1731–1764. Poet and satirist. Friend of John Wilkes and co-author of *The North Briton*.

WILLIAM COWPER 1731–1800. Poet. (*Romney* 1792).

GEORGE COLMAN 1732–1794. Playwright and producer.

RICHARD CUMBERLAND 1732–1811. Dramatist. Original of Sheridan's Fretful Plagiary.

WARREN HASTINGS 1732–1818. Governor-General of Bengal. Acquitted of cruelty and corruption after an 8-year trial, 1795. (*Reynolds* 1766).

JOHN HINCHLIFFE 1732–1794. Head Master. Master of Trinity and Bishop of Peterborough.

RICHARD HILL 1732–1808. Champion of Whitefield and the Calvinistic Methodists.

SAMUEL SMITH 1732–1808. Head Master.

ELIJAH IMPEY 1732–1809. Chief Justice of Bengal.

NEVIL MASKELYNE, F.R.S. 1732–1811. Astronomer-Royal. Established the Nautical Almanack.

HENRY JENNINGS 1732–1819. Collector and gambler. Three times jailed for debt; three collections sold to defray his bills.

PHILIP STANHOPE 1733–1768. Natural son of Earl of Chesterfield and recipient of the famous letters.

CHARLES LENNOX, 3rd Duke of Richmond and Lennox 1735–1806. Field-Marshal. Politician. Patron of the arts: founded a school for painting and sculpture in Richmond House, Whitehall.

JOHN TRUSSLER 1735–1820. Eccentric divine and literary compiler.

JOHN MONTRESOR 1736–1799. Military engineer. Prominent in campaigns in America and Canada.

JOHN HORNE TOOKE 1736–1812. Upholder of public justice and popular rights. Supporter of the American Revolution. Founder of the Constitutional Society. Acquitted of high treason 1794. (*Houston* c. 1768).

EDWARD GIBBON, F.R.S. 1737–1794. Historian. (*Walton* c. 1773).

WILLIAM HENRY CAVENDISH-BENTINCK, 3rd Duke of Portland 1738–1809. First Lord of Treasury (twice), Home Secretary, instrumental in Act of Union 1801, Knight of the Garter.

JOHN BRAITHWAITE 1739–1803. Captured Pondicherrry 1793. C in C Madras army.

WILLIAM VINCENT 1739–1815. Head Master and Dean. Preserver of Vincent Square. (*Eldridge*).

WILLOUGHBY BERTIE, 4th Earl of Abingdon 1740–1799. Supporter of Wilkes, and of the American and French Revolutions.

AUGUSTUS TOPLADY 1741–1778. Champion of extreme Calvinism. Editor of the Gospel Magazine. Hymn writer *Rock of Ages*.

ARTHUR MIDDLETON 1742–1787. Signatory of Declaration of Independence. Framed constitution for State of Carolina, but declined Governorship.

WILLIAM DRAYTON 1742–1779. Chief Justice and President of South Carolina.

ROBERT SMYTH 1744–1802. Friend of Tom Paine, and supporter of the French Revolution. Lived in France, a member of the British Revolutionary Club. Renounced his title.

JOHN BLAKE 1745–1773. Naturalist, collector of plants and seeds in China. Died at Canton.

JOHN SACKVILLE, 3rd Duke of Dorset 1745–1799. Member of the Hambledon cricket club, and one of the Committee who drew up the original laws of the Marylebone Club.

EUSEBY CLEAVER 1745–1819. Archbishop of Dublin.

CHARLES PINCKNEY 1746–1825. ADC to Washington 1777. A delegate to the Convention which framed the American constitution. U.S. Minister to France. Defeated by Jefferson in 1804 in contest for Presidency.

GEORGE HARRIS, 1st Baron 1746–1829. General and Governor of Madras.

JEREMY BENTHAM 1748–1832. Philosopher. (*Pickersgill* 1829).

WILLIAM HICKEY 1749–1830? 'Gentleman Attorney' in Calcutta. Author of *Memoirs of William Hickey*. (*Thomas* 1819).

JOHN RANDOLPH 1749–1813. Professor of Poetry, Greek, Moral Philosophy and Divinity at Oxford. Bishop of Oxford, Bangor and London.

THOMAS PINCKNEY 1750–1828. U.S. Minister to England 1792. Member of Congress. Governor of South Carolina.

H. W. BUNBURY 1750–1811. Caricaturist.

RICHARD TICKELL 1751–1793. Dramatist; pamphleteer, friend of Sheridan.

GEORGE WYNDHAM, 3rd Earl of Egremont 1751–1837. Patron of Turner and racehorse owner. Won Derby and Oaks each five times.

CHARLES KNYVETT 1752–1822. Organist, singer, concert promoter.

JAMES BLAND-BURGES 1752–1824. Politician; man of letters; supporter of Hastings and Wilberforce.

RICHARD RELHAN 1754–1823. Botanist; founder fellow of the Linnean Society. Editor of Tacitus.

EVERARD HOME 1756–1832. Professor of Anatomy and Surgery. Surgeon to George III and IV.

SAMUEL BENTHAM 1757–1831. Brother of Jeremy. Superintendant of Potemkin's shipbuilding yard at Kritchev; Inspector-General of Navy Works 1795–1807.

EDWARD HARCOURT 1757–1847. Archbishop of York 1808–47.

CHARLES ABBOT, Viscount Colchester 1757–1829. Speaker of the Commons 1802–1817.

ELIAB HARVEY 1758–1830. Admiral. Commander of the *Fighting Temeraire* at Trafalgar.

GEORGE LEVESON GOWER, 1st Duke of Sutherland 1758–1833. Politician; supporter of the Reform Bill and Catholic Emancipation.

HOME RIGGS POPHAM 1760–1820. Rear-Admiral. Devised Navy code of signals used at Trafalgar.

JOHN WINGFIELD 1760–1825. Head Master.

CHARLES ASGILL 1762–1823. Soldier in America, Flanders, Ireland. General 1814.

GEORGE COLMAN THE YOUNGER 1762–1836. Playwright and theatre manager.

WILLIAM HAY 1762–1839. Magistrate at Peterloo.

WILLIAM FRANCKLIN 1763–1839. Orientalist.

FREDERIC REYNOLDS 1764–1841. Playwright. Won short-term success with some of his hundred plays. Contemptuously dismissed by Byron.

FRANCIS RUSSELL, 5th Duke of Bedford 1765–1802. Friend and supporter of Fox. Subject of Burke's *Letter to a Noble Lord* (1796). Patron of turf, thrice winner of the Derby; agricultural innovator.

HARMAN BLENNERHASSET 1765–1831. Emigrated to U.S.A. on account of his republican principles; arrested for treason; cotton-grower in Mississippi; lawyer in Montreal.

THOMAS BRUCE, 7th Earl of Elgin 1766–1841. Ambassador to Constantinople. Bringer of the Elgin Marbles to Britain.

ROBERT GROSVENOR, 1st Marquis of Westminster 1767–1845. Art collector, racehorse owner; laid out Belgravia.

CHARLES ARBUTHNOT 1767–1850. Diplomat, politician, confidential friend of Wellington.

WALTER FAIRLEES 1769–1825. Whig; prominent in anti-slavery movement; cattle breeder; friend and patron of Turner.

WILLIAM CAREY 1769–1846. Head Master. Bishop of Exeter and St Asaph.

JOHN BECKER 1770–1848. Social reformer.

FRANCIS BURDETT 1770–1844. Radical and parliamentary reformer.

HENRY PAGET, 1st Marquis of Anglesey 1768–1854. Lieutenant-General. Commanded cavalry at Corunna 1808; cavalry and horse artillery at Waterloo, where he lost a leg. Field-Marshal 1846. Lord Lieutenant of Ireland. (*Eldridge* 1808).

JOHN BYNG, 1st Earl of Strafford 1772–1860. Commander of 2nd Brigade at Waterloo. C in C Ireland. Field-Marshal.

RUFANE DONKIN 1772–1841. Surveyor-General of the Ordnance. Founder fellow of Royal Geographical Society.

WILLIAM PITT AMHERST, 1st Earl 1773–1857. Diplomat. Governor-General of Bengal.

STAPLETON COTTON, 1st Viscount Combermere 1773–1865. Major-General and cavalry commander under Wellington; Field-Marshal.

ROBERT SOUTHEY 1774–1843. Poet Laureate 1813. Essayist and biographer of Nelson. (*Eldridge* 1804).

JAMES VAN MILLINGEN 1774–1845. Imprisoned in Paris during the French Revolution. Banker. Purchaser of Italian antiquities which he sold to European museums.

WILLIAM CAVENDISH-BENTINCK 1774–1839. General. Governor General of India.

BENJAMIN WYATT 1775–1850. Architect.

MATTHEW 'MONK' LEWIS 1775–1818. Gothic novelist; died at sea after visiting his Jamaica estates to attend to the welfare of his slaves.

EDWARD PAGET 1775–1849. 2nd i/c to Welleseley in Peninsular.

JOHN KIDD 1775–1851. Professor of Chemistry; Regius Professor of Medicine.

ROBERT BLOSSET 1776–1823. Chief Justice in Bengal 1821; died at Calcutta.

ROBERT SOMERSET 1776–1842. General. Commander of the Household Cavalry at Waterloo.

ROBERT WILSON 1777–1849. General. An active and successful soldier for over 50 years. Much honoured by European powers, his merits were largely ignored in England.

WILLIAM GAGE 1777–1862. Admiral of the Fleet. C in C East Indies, Lisbon, Plymouth.

WILLIAM PAGE 1778–1819. Head Master.

CHARLES DOYLE 1778–1842. Major-General. Fought with Spanish army in Catalonia 1818–14.

JAMES BOSWELL 1778–1822. Son of Johnson's biographer; editor of Shakespeare.

JOHN CONGREAVE 1779–1824. Geologist, theologian, philologist.

HENRY PETTY-FITZMAURICE, 3rd Marquis of Lansdowne 1780–1863. Cabinet minister. Opposed slave trade; supported emancipation of Catholics and Jews.

FREDERICK MABERLEY 1781–1860. Eccentric and zealous Protestant. Opposed to Catholic emancipation and Amendment of the Poor Law; ejected from the Lords while trying to impeach Wellington.

ROBERT DICK 1786–1846. Commander of 42nd Highlanders at Waterloo. C in C Madras. Killed fighting the Sikhs.

JOHN CAM HOBHOUSE, Lord Broughton 1786–1869. Politician. Friend and executor of Byron.

GEORGE HARLOW 1787–1819. Painter.

FITZROY SOMERSET, 1st Baron Raglan 1788–1855. Field-Marshal. Served in the Peninsular War; lost his right arm at Waterloo. C in C in the Crimea. Died in camp before Sebastopol. (*Fenton* 1855).

GEORGE FINCH-HATTON, 9th Earl of Winchelsea 1791–1858. Extreme Protestant. Duelled with Wellington in Battersea Fields, 1829, over Catholic emancipation.

JAMES STIRLING 1791–1865. Admiral. C in C China and East Indies. Governor of Western Australia 1829–39.

JAMES GRAHAM 1792–1861. Home Secretary 1841–6. Unpopular for tampering with letters of foreign refugees.

SYDNEY COTTON 1792–1874. Brigadier; commander at Peshawar in the Indian Mutiny. Writer on N.W. Frontier.

JOHN RUSSELL, 1st Earl 1792–1878. Introduced the Reform Bill 1831. Leader of the Whigs in the Commons 1835. Home Secretary, First Lord of the Treasury 1846–52, 1865–6, Foreign Secretary, President of the Council. (*Dickinson* 1855).

JOHN GORDON LENNOX 1793–1873. ADC to Wellington at Waterloo.

CHARLES LONGLEY 1794–1868. Archbishop of York and Canterbury.

HENRY ROUS 1795–1877. Admiral. Sailed his frigate 1500 miles without a rudder, and badly holed, in 1835. Steward of the Jockey Club and dictator of the turf in the last 40 years of his life.

JOHN MYTTON 1796–1834. Sportsman, spendthrift, reckless joker and adventurer. Squandered his fortune; drank 6 bottles of port a day; died of d.t.'s in the King's Bench prison.

EDWARD GIBBON WAKEFIELD 1796–1862. Influential theorist and reformer of colonisation: Canada, Australia, and New Zealand, to which he emigrated.

WILLIAM DE ROS, 3rd Baron 1797–1874. Quartermaster General in the Crimea.

GEORGE ELLIS 1797–1833. Historian; promoter of the National Gallery.

JOHN WROTTESLEY, 2nd Baron 1798–1867. Astronomer. President of the Royal Society.

GEORGE KEPPEL, 6th Earl of Albemarle 1799–1891. Expelled from school for going to the theatre. General; served at Waterloo.

HENRY BARNARD 1799–1857. Commander and Chief of Staff, Crimea. Commander, Indian Mutiny. Died of cholera during siege of Delhi.

GEORGE BINGHAM, 3rd Earl of Lucan 1800–1888. Field Marshal. Cavalry commander in the Crimea.

JOHN DARBY 1800–1882. Left Church to join Plymouth Brethren; founded his own sect (Darbyites) 1845.

VINCENT COTTEN 1801–1863. Sportsman. Gambled away his estates, and earned a living driving a London–Brighton stagecoach.

JOHN JERVIS 1802–1856. Attorney-General; Chief Justice of Common Pleas.

RICHARD WILLIAMSON 1802–1865. Head Master.

BENJAMIN HALL 1802–1867. Commissioner of Works and Public Buildings. 'Big Ben' named after him in 1856.

BELFORD HINTON WILSON 1804–1858. ADC to General Bolivar 1823–30.

CHARLES BADHAM 1805–1857. Naturalist.

GILBERT A'BECKETT 1811–1856. Comic journalist. A founder of *Punch*.

HENRY MAYHEW 1812–1887. Ran away from school during the Challenge 1826. Philanthropic journalist. Joint editor of *Punch*. Author of *London Labour and the London Poor* (1864).

LORD GEORGE PAGET 1813–1880. Lieutenant General. Commander of Dragoons at Balaclava, and Light Brigade at Inkerman.

GEORGE COTTON 1813–1866. 'Young Master' of *Tom Brown's Schooldays*. Head Master of Marlborough; Bishop of Calcutta. Drowned in the Ganges.

AMBROSE ST JOHN 1815–1875. Lifelong companion of Newman, and buried in the same grave.

WILLIAM BRETT, Viscount Esher 1815–1899. Master of the Rolls.

GEORGE WEBBE DASENT 1817–1896. Scandinavian scholar; translator of sagas.

JAMES FROUDE 1818–1894. Historian. (*Reid* 1881)

WILLIAM VAUX 1818–1885. Orientalist and numismatist.

CHARLES GORDON-LENNOX, 6th Duke of Richmond and 1st Duke of Gordon 1818–1903. Lord President of Council and Secretary for Scotland. Agriculturalist.

WILLIAM BEDFORD 1826–1905. Genealogist and sportsman. Founder of Free Foresters 1856.

WALTER SEVERN 1830–1904. Prominent figure in the art and craft movement from 1857; furniture, art, needlework, watercolours.

CLEMENTS MARKHAM 1830–1916. Traveller. President of the Royal Geographical Society.

GEORGE (G.A.) HENTY 1832–1902. Purveyor of the Forces. War correspondent of *The Standard*. Author of over 80 popular books for boys. Died on his yacht in Weymouth Harbour.

C. L. EASTLAKE 1833–1906. Keeper of National Gallery.

EDWARD POYNTER 1836–1919. Director of National Gallery. President of Royal Academy.

HENRY EDWARDS 1837–1884. Dean of Bangor; noted opponent of the habit of tea drinking.

FRANK MCLEAN 1837–1904. Astronomer and collector of manuscripts and printed books. Founded Isaac Newton Scholarships in Astronomy at Cambridge, and left his collection to the Fitzwilliam.

JOHN COWELL 1838–1867. Early mountaineer and secretary of the Alpine Club. Taste formed by climbing the Victoria Tower while under construction.

JOHN BIDDULPH 1840–1921. Explorer of the Hindu Kush.

EDWARD KNIGHT 1852–1925. Traveller, sailor; war correspondent.

CHARLES LUSH 1853–1930. Justice of King's Bench.

RALEIGH EGERTON 1860–1931. Lieutenant-General. Served in Bengal, Punjab and on the Western Front.

WILLIAM PAGE 1861–1934. Editor: *Victorian History of Counties of England*.

HENRY BATTERSBY 1862–? War correspondent in Boer War and World War I.

CECIL HURST 1870–1963. Legal adviser to Foreign Office; negotiator Versailles Treaty 1919; President of Court of Justice at The Hague.

R. F. DOHERTY 1872–1910. England tennis champion (with his brother, see below).

EDWARD MARSH 1872–1953. Literary editor.

ARTHUR MARTIN-LEAKE 1874–1953. Twice winner of V.C.: Boer War and World War I.

H. L. DOHERTY 1875–1919. England tennis champion.

KEPPEL CRESWELL 1879–1974. Professor of Moslem Art and Archeology.

RUSSEL REYNOLDS 1880–1964. Radiologist. Professor: Royal College of Surgeons.

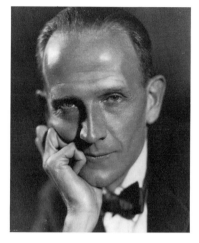

A. A. MILNE 1882–1953. Author and journalist.

WILFRID GREENE 1883–1952. Master of the Rolls.

GEORGE KENNEDY BELL 1883–1958. Bishop of Chichester.

HARRY ST JOHN PHILBY 1885–1960. Arabian explorer and scholar.

JOHN SPEDAN LEWIS 1885–1963. Founder of John Lewis Partnership.

HENRY TIZARD 1885–1959. Scientist and inventor.

STEPHEN MCKENNA 1888–1967. Novelist.

WILHELM HAMEL 1889–1914. Early aviator. Winner of the Aerial Derby 1912 and 1913.

JOHN DAVIDSON, 1st Viscount 1889–1970. Conservative politician.

EDGAR ADRIAN, 1st Baron 1889–1977. President of the Royal Society; Master of Trinity and Chancellor of Cambridge University.

ADRIAN BOULT 1889–1984. Conductor.

LAWRENCE TANNER 1890–1979. Antiquary. Historian of Westminster. Librarian and Keeper of the Abbey Muniments.

R. M. BARRINGTON-WARD 1891–1948. Editor of The Times.

H. M. HAKE 1892–1951. Director of the National Portrait Gallery.

DOUGLAS JERROLD 1893–1964. Author.

OLIVER LYTTELTON, 1st Viscount Chandos 1893–1972. Member of War Cabinet. Colonial Secretary. Chairman of National Theatre Board.

MEREDITH FRAMPTON 1894–1984. Artist.

JOHN AINSWORTH DAVIS 1895–1976. Olympic athlete.

STEPHEN POTTER 1900–1969. Author.

PHILIP HENDY 1900–1980. Director of the National Gallery.

ROY HARROD 1900–1978. Economist.

PHILIP REA 1900–1981. Liberal peer; party leader in the Lords.

EWAN MONTAGU 1901–1985. Lawyer. Author of The Man Who Never Was.

DONALD HARDEN 1901–. Director of London Museum.

HUMFRY PAYNE 1902–1936. Director of British School of Archeology, Athens.

A. L. D. HASKELL 1903–1980. Director of Royal Ballet School.

CHARLES SCOTT 1903–1946. Winner of England–Australia air-race in 1934.

PATRICK HAMILTON 1904–1972. Novelist.

ARTHUR CROSS 1904–. Lord Justice of Appeal. Lord of Appeal in Ordinary.

GLEN BYAM SHAW 1904–1986. Actor and director.

JOHN GIELGUD 1904–. Actor and director.

DAVID ENSOR 1906–1987. Lawyer, actor, Labour M.P. 1964–70.

ESMOND KNIGHT 1906–1987. Actor.

PHILIP MAGNUS 1906–. Historian.

H. R. A. ('JUMBO') EDWARDS 1906–1972. Oarsman and rowing coach.

MAX AITKEN 1910–1985. Journalist and newspaper proprietor.

GERALD ELLISON 1910–. Bishop of Chester and London.

H. A. R. ('KIM') PHILBY 1912–. Journalist. Defected to U.S.S.R. 1963.

ANGUS WILSON 1913–. Novelist.

NORMAN PARKINSON 1913–. Photographer.

MICHAEL ARGYLE 1915–. Judge.

FRANK BYERS 1915–1984. Politician; leader of the Liberal Party in the Lords.

JOHN FREEMAN 1915–. Diplomat; journalist; broadcaster.

ROBERT CARR, Life Peer 1916–. Politician; Home Secretary.

ASHLEY BRAMALL 1916–. G.L.C. Leader I.L.E.A.

BRIAN URQUHART 1919–. United Nations Secretariat.

FRANCIS NOEL-BAKER 1920–. M.P.

DAVID PEARS 1921–. Philosopher.

PETER USTINOV 1921–. Actor, writer, director.

NICHOLAS KATZENBACH 1922–. U.S. Attorney General; Under Secretary of State.

MICHAEL FLANDERS 1922–1975. Writer and entertainer.

DONALD SWANN 1923–. Musician and entertainer.

RICHARD WOLLHEIM 1923–. Philosopher.

MICHAEL HAVERS 1923–. Attorney-General.

MICHAEL HAMBURGER 1924–. German scholar and translator.

TONY BENN 1925–. M.P. Secretary of State for Energy.

PETER BROOK 1925–. Theatre director.

ANTHONY SAMPSON 1926–. Author and Journalist.

NIGEL LAWSON 1932–. Chancellor of the Exchequer.

NICHOLAS EDWARDS 1934–. M.P. Secretary of State for Wales.

ANTHONY HOWARD 1934–. Journalist.

ROGER NORRINGTON 1934–. Musician.

SIMON GRAY 1936–. Novelist and playwright.

ANTHONY STEEN 1939–. M.P. Founder of 'Shelter'

DOMINIC HARROD 1940–. Economist; broadcaster; journalist.

NICHOLAS HUMPHREY 1943–. Psychologist, writer, broadcaster.

PETER BOTTOMLEY 1944– . M.P.

DAN TOPOLSKI 1945–. Oarsman and rowing coach.

ANTHONY PEEBLES 1946–. Pianist.

ANDREW LLOYD-WEBBER 1948–. Composer and producer.

STEPHEN POLIAKOFF 1952–. Playwright.

TIM SEBASTIAN 1952–. Broadcaster.

NIGEL PLANER 1953–. Actor.

RICHARD BLACKFORD 1954–. Composer.

GEORGE BENJAMIN 1960–. Composer.

ANDREW HUXLEY 1917–. F.R.S. Master of Trinity College, Cambridge.

10

CHRONOLOGY

HEAD MASTERS, PUPILS,	EVENTS	HEAD MASTERS, PUPILS,	EVENTS
1540 JOHN ADAMS	1540 Dissolution of Benedictine Monastery	1622 LAMBERT OSBALDSTON	1624 Dean Williams's benefaction
	1541 Statutes establishing Collegiate Church and See of Westminster	Abraham Cowley (1629–36)	
1543 ALEXANDER NOWELL	1543 Henry VIII endows the College with lands	1638 RICHARD BUSBY	1638 Osbaldston sentenced to pillory by Star Chamber: goes into hiding
	c. 1545 Refectory demolished: stone used to build Somerset House	Christopher Wren (1641–46)	1641 Purchase of muskets and powder for College
	1550 Abolition of Bishopric of Westminster		1642 Scholars defend Abbey against a Puritan mob
1555 NICHOLAS UDALL	1556–58 Restoration of monastery	John Dryden (c. 1643–50)	1645 Ordinance of Lords and Commons: committee appointed to run School and Almshouses
1558 JOHN PASSEY	1558 17th November: Accession of Elizabeth I	John Locke (c. 1645–52)	1649 Execution of Charles I: Busby leads School in prayers for the King on the day of his beheading.
1560 WILLIAM?	1560 New charter for 'The College'	Robert Hooke (c. 1650)	Deans and Chapters abolished: Act for the Continuance of the School and Almshouses
	1561 Elizabethan Statutes establish links with Christ Church, Oxford, and Trinity, Cambridge		1657–58 Busby's quarrel with Edward Bagshawe
	1562 First Election Dinner		1658 'Majesty Scutcheon' snatched by Robert Uvedale, Scholar, at Cromwell's funeral
1563 JOHN RANDALL	1563 First recorded retreat from plague to Putney		c. 1659 Busby Library built
Richard Hakluyt (1564–70)	1564 Elizabeth attends Latin Plays		
1564 THOMAS BROWNE		1660 Busby, Prebendary and Treasurer of Wells	1660 Restoration of Charles II
1570 FRANCIS HOWLYN	1570 Permanent refuge from plague secured at Chiswick		1661 John Evelyn visits the Election
			1662–65 Ashburnham House built
1572 EDWARD GRANT		1663 THOMAS KNIPE, Second Master	1665 Great Plague: School adjourned for six months
1575 WILLIAM CAMDEN (Second Master)	1576 First public theatre in London		1666 Fire of London. Dean Dolben and Scholars save St Dunstan's in the East
	c. 1580 Present gallery and tables added to College Hall		
Ben Jonson (c. 1585)	1587 Verses presented to the Queen on her New Year visit	1672 Busby, Archdeacon of Westminster	1679 Murder of a bailiff by Westminster boys
1593 WILLIAM CAMDEN	1594 Lord Burghley's benefaction		c. 1680 Ceiling of Busby Library added
1599 RICHARD IRELAND	1599 Monk's Dormitory first used as Schoolroom		1685 Westminster boys first formally attend a Coronation
George Herbert (1605–8)	1601–5 Lancelot Andrewes, Dean, begins to teach Scholars Hebrew	1695 THOMAS KNIPE	1704 First recorded Latin Play in old Scholars' Dormitory
	1605 Gunpowder plot: Royalist pamphlet by Edward Hawes, Scholar	1711 ROBERT FREIND	1711 Jonathan Swift turned away from Election Dinner
	1608 'Great dearth of all things'		1711–22 Chapter dispute about the site of the new Dormitory
1610 JOHN WILSON	1610 Richard Ireland flees to France because of a 'bruit' about his religion		1716 Edmund Curll, publisher, tossed in a blanket and flogged
	1621 William Laud, Prebendary of Westminster		1722 Burlington lays foundation stone of new Dormitory
		1733 JOHN NICOLL	1729 Scholars occupy new Dormitory

HEAD MASTERS, PUPILS,	EVENTS	HEAD MASTERS, PUPILS,	EVENTS
William Cowper (1742–49) Warren Hastings (1743–49) Edward Gibbon (1748–50)	1731 Fire in Ashburnham House: Cottonian library rescued and stored in Old Dormitory 1734 Burlington's Arch in Little Dean's Yard 1739 Ashburnham House becomes Chapter residence 1746 First recorded cricket match: Old Westminsters v. Old Etonians 1750 Grant family begins to manage a boarding house		1837 Westminster's victory over Eton at rowing hastens death of William IV 1837 'Murderous scream of recognition' from Scholars at Victoria's Coronation 1838–39 Hot water pipes and gaslight installed 'Up School' 1841 Low point of school's fortunes: 67 boys
1753 WILLIAM MARKHAM Jeremy Bentham (1755–60)	1753 First recorded Pancake Greaze 1756 Dean's Yard improvements. Old Granary demolished; terrace built on south side for boarding houses 1760 Bicentennial celebrations	1846 HENRY GEORGE LIDDELL	1846 Dean Buckland's reforms: open cloister of College enclosed; sanatorium built 1847 Treacle puddings thrown at the cook 1848 Chartist unrest: boys enrolled as special constables 1849 Cholera epidemic when drains are dug out
1764 JOHN HINCHLIFFE 1764 SAMUEL SMITH	1779 Dean's Yard Affray: eleven boys on trial 1783 Warren Hastings and other OW in the East India Company send silver cup to the School 1786 Rebellion in the School: Francis Burdett felled by Head Master's cudgel	1855 CHARLES BRODERICK SCOTT	1855 Last wholly oral 'Challenge' 1858 Prince Albert and Prince of Wales attend Latin Play 1861 Crimean War/Indian Mutiny Memorial Column 1861 Gymnasium built for School's Tercentenary 1864 Report of Public Schools Commission published 1865 Bloodshed at the Greaze 1868 Public Schools Act gives Westminster independence 1870s Embanking of the Thames threatens rowing at Westminster 1873 Closed scholarships at Christ Church and Trinity opened to Town Boys 1875 Last fighting 'mill' in Cloisters 1876 'Challenge' opened to candidates from outside the School 1877 'Home Boarders' house 1881 Ashburnham House purchased on death of Lord John Thynne; new day boy house ('Ashburnham') started 1883 'Turle's house' acquired; building of classrooms on the site
1788 WILLIAM VINCENT Robert Southey (1788–92)	1790 Little Dean's Yard terrace built 1792 Southey expelled for his articles in *The Flagellant* 1796 First cricket match against Eton at Hounslow Heath		
1802 JOHN WINGFIELD			
1803 WILLIAM CAREY	1803 Grosvenor boys shoot their own snipe in what is now Belgrave Square Westminster boys help extinguish fire in Abbey roof c. 1810 Street battles against 'skies' get under way 1810 Vincent Square secured as playing field 1814 Rebuilding in brick of crumbling walls of School	1883 WILLIAM GUNION RUTHERFORD A. A. Milne (1893–1900)	1883 First non-classical curriculum 1884 Rowing abolished 1896 Rebuilding of Rigauds (1, Little Dean's Yard)
1815 WILLIAM PAGE	1815 Vincent Square enclosed c. 1815 Competitive rowing begins	1901 JAMES GOW Adrian Boult (1901–8) Edgar Adrian (1903–8)	1902 Cadet Corps founded 1905–06 First Science building in Great College St 1908 Suffragette demonstrations cause closing of the gates Resumption of rowing 1919 George V and Queen Mary attend Pancake Greaze 1921 Boathouse at Putney purchased
1819 EDMUND GOODENOUGH	Ditch-leaping at Battersea on St David's Day (March 1st) for much of the century 1827 Old Lodge at Vincent Square built		
1828 RICHARD WILLIAMSON	1834 Fire destroys old Palace of Westminster 1834 William IV tricked into attending Latin Play		

HEAD MASTERS, PUPILS,	EVENTS	HEAD MASTERS, PUPILS,	EVENTS
1919 HAROLD COSTLEY-WHITE	1925 New boarding house (Busby's) opened on Dean's Yard terrace 1926 General Strike: boys volunteer for transport and printing duties 1933 Playing fields acquired at Grove Park, South London 1936–39 Demolition of Dean's Yard terrace and building of Church House. New premises for Busby's		1943 Under School started in Little Dean's Yard 1945 Return to Westminster
		1950 WALTER HAMILTON	1950 George VI reopens College 1951 Busby Library restored 1955 Under School moves to Eccleston Square 1956 New boarding house (Liddells) opened 1957–58 Rebuilding of Science block
1937 JOHN CHRISTIE	1937 King and Queen attend Latin Play 1938 Munich crisis: evacuation to Lancing 1939 Second evacuation to Lancing and Hurstpierpoint 1940 Move from Lancing to Exeter for Summer Term 1940 Move back to London completed; blitz begins next day. School suspended until November 1940–45 Westminster in Herefordshire 1940 Busby Library destroyed Head Master's secretary killed in air raid 1941 School and College destroyed in air raid	1958 JOHN CARLETON 1970 JOHN RAE – 1986 1986 DAVID SUMMERSCALE	1960 Quatercentenary and visit by the Queen 1967 First girl pupil 1973 Girls first become full members of the School 1976 New day house (Drydens) 1981 Girls' boarding house opened in Barton St 1981 Acquisition of new Under School (Adrian House) in Vincent Square 1986 Acquisition of new science building in Smith Square

INDEX

Titles, honorifics and so on are omitted unless required for identification. The names of Head Masters of Westminster are printed in capitals, and of Deans of Westminster are followed by 'Dean'. Figures in bold print refer to illustrations.

Abbot, Charles, Viscount Colchester, 70, 135
ADAMS, John, **16**, 18, 19
Adrian, Edgar 79, **138**
Albert, H.R.H. Prince, 10, 52, 66
Alexander III, Pope, 15
Andrewes, Lancelot, Dean, 28
Angel, John, 95
Architectural Review, 124
Ashburnham House, 12, 14, **21, 33,** 43, **65, 74,** 75f., **79, 80,** 85, 95, 97, 104, 119, 122–4, **124–5**
Atterbury, Francis, Dean, 27, 46f., 50, 119
Austen, Jane, 65

Bagshawe, Edward, Under Master, 37
Baker, William, 16
Barber, John, 56
Barrington-Ward, R.M., 86, 138
Benn, Tony, 83, 99, 139
Bentham, Jeremy, 77, 135
Bentley, Richard, 123
Bill, W., Dean, 21
Bingham, George, 3rd Earl of Lucan, 62, 137
Booth, Barton, 43, 128, 132
Boston, Abbot William, 18
Boswell, James, 59, 136
Bourne, Vincent, 55
Bowle, John, 87
Brettingham, R.F., **120f.,** 122
Buckland, William, Dean, 35, 66
Bull, J.S., 65
Burdett, Francis, 56, 64, 135
Burghley, Lord, 27, 28, 33, 119
Burlington: Arch, **49, 55,** 116
  collonnade, 66, 116
  Dormitory, 34, **46f.,** 51, 100, 119
BUSBY, Richard, **30, 32,** 31–44, 51, 66, 77, 102, 117–9, 130
  Library, 10, 37, **38,** 92, 95, 100, 119
Busby's, **47,** 86f., 142.

cadet corps, 80, 87, **89,** 95, 99, 106, 141
Caithness, Lady, 34
CAMDEN, William, 27–9, **32**
Campbell, J.B., 65
CAREY, William, 62, 135
Carleton, Dudley, 120, 129
CARLETON, John, iv, v, 82, 86, 88f., 98, **101,** 102–6, 111
Carnegie, Canon, 126
Challenge, 13, 32, **38,** 54, 69

Challis, R.G., 64
Charles I, 35, 36f.
Charles II, 44
Charterhouse Match, 72
Chiswick, 25, 34, 122
CHRISTIE, John Traill, 88–101, **89, 99**
Clarendon Commission on the Public Schools, 62, 66, 70, 74–6, 116, 126, 128
College Hall, **13,** 14, 23, 26, **65, 79, 80,** 92, 113ff., 124
College House, 24
Colman, George, viii, 57, 59, 134
Cooper, Allen, 65
COSTLEY-WHITE, Harold, 85–8
Cotton, Robert, 28, 129
Cowper, William, 60, **134**
Cranmer, Thomas, 18
Creighton, Robert, 44
Cromwell, Oliver, 37
Crow, James, 36
Cumberland, Richard, 45, 134
curriculum, 17, 21f., 32, 39f., 65, 75, 77, 80, 84, 108
Curll, Edmund, 56

Dasent, George Webbe, 77, 137
Davidson, John, 1st Viscount, 90, 138
Dee, John, 28
Denny, Anthony, 18
de Ros, William, 63, 137
Dickens, Charles, (Pickwick Papers), 11
Dickson, Robert, B., 62
Doblen, John, Dean, 42f., 130
Don, Alan, Dean, 98
Drayton, William, 57, 135
dress (school uniform), **10,** 11, 83, 90, 92, 95, 99
Dryden, John, 34f., **40, 130**

Eady, Wilfred, 92
Edith, Queen, 14
Edward the Confessor, 14, 118
Edward VII, 52, 73
Edward VIII, **78**
Election, 22, 26f., 32, 36, 38, 40, 48, 51, 78, 102, 111, 115
Elizabeth I, 21, 22, 31, **32,** 91, 115, 117
Ellis, John, 43
Erskine, Lord, 50
Eton, 17, 49, 62; boat-races 65, 72, 80; cricket 57; curriculum 21f., 39

evacuation, Rossall 88; Lancing 88f., Exeter 91; Herefordshire 11, 92–6, **93,** 142
Evelyn, John, 40

Fawcett, Thomas, 59f.
Fisher, Preedy, 92
Fitzstephen, W., 13, 14
Flanders, Michael, 91, 139
Fortescue, John, 122
Freeman, John, 83, 138
FREIND, Robert, 114, 120

Garten, Hugo, 99
Gasker, Guy, 126
Gay, John, 54
Gentleman's Magazine, 40
George I, 46, 119
George III, 49, 62
George V, 44, **78,** 141
George VI, **78,** 88, **89, 101**
Gibbon, Edward, 40, 56, **134**
Gielgud, John, 27, 79, 83, **138**
Ginger, 32, 70
Gladstone, W.E., 76
Godley, Arthur, 39
GOODENOUGH, Edmund, 64–6, 70f.
Goodman, Gabriel, Dean, 21, **24,** 25, 27
GOW, James, 36, 44, 62, 73, **78,** 79–82
GRANT, Edward, 27, 129
Grant's, 25, 56, **69, 81,** 90, 92, 94, 99, 102, 122

Hailsham, Lord, 27
Halley, J.M.W., 124
Hamilton, Archibald, 58
HAMILTON, Walter, **101f.**
Hannes, Edward, 26f.
Harley, Edward, 119
Harrod, Roy, 79, 138
Hastings, Warren, 57, 134
Havers, Michael, 27, 139
Hebbone, Odnell (or Odrick), **16,** 18
Henry III, 128
Henry VIII, 17
Henry, Philip, 42, 130
Henty, G.A., 64, 137
Herland, Hugh, **13,** 14, 114
HINCHLIFFE, John, 51, 134
Hooke, Robert, 37, 119, 131
Husbands, Sam, 57

Ingram, 'Bunk', Under Master, 70

143

Ingulphus, Chronicle of, 14
IRELAND, Richard, 31, 129

Jackson, Cyril, 61
Jackson, T.G., 122
James II, 44
Jeffreys, George, 27, **131**
Jekyll, Edward, 65
Johnson, Samuel, 126
Jonson, Ben, 23, 25, 27, 28, **29**, 129

Knight, Donald, 85
KNIPE, Thomas, 48, 102, 113, 131
Kyrkeham, Thomas, 16

Lamb, William, Viscount
    Melbourne, 57
Latin Play, 13, 25f., 32, 45, **50,**
    51-4, 72, 78, 83f., 90, 98, 100f.,
    115, 119
Laud, William, 32
LIDDELL, H.G., 10, 32, 66, 74, 77,
    78
Liddell's, 102, 116
Litlyngton, Abbot Nicholas, **12,**
    14, 35, 114, 116
Lloyd, Pierson, Under Master, 48,
    60
Locke, John, **38, 104, 131**
Longley, Charles, 114, 137

Mansfield, Lord, 54
Mar, Earl of, 50
MARKHAM, William, **47,** 51, 55,
    57, 87, 116, 122, 133
Mecey, Miss, 92
Middleton, Arthur, 57, 135
Mills, Henry, 59
Milman, Canon, 73, 76
Mortymer, George, 16
Munich, 89

Neile, Richard, 23
Newborough, John, 16
NICOLL, John, 48, 51, 59f., 132
NOWELL, Alexander, 18, **32,** 52
O'Brien, George, 70
Ortelius, 28
OSBALDSTON, Lambert, 31f.,
    129
Owen, Richard, 8

Pancake Greaze, 13, 44, 77, **98,**
    111, 118
Paget, Clarence, 64
Payne, John, 16
Pearce, Zachary, Dean, 51
Pepys, Samuel, 43, 122
Pinckney – Charles and Thomas,
    57, 135
Pitt, William, 42
Pope, Alexander, 42, 54, 56
Powell, Enoch, 27
Prag, Adolf, 99
Price, Owen, 37
Prideaux, Humphrey, 39, 43, 131
Public Advertiser, 51, 56
Public Schools Commission – v.
    Clarendon

Radyclyffe, C.W., **33, 46, 115, 120**
RAE, John, v, 106–11
Raglan Lord (Fitzroy Smerset), 63,
    136
Rawes, Francis, 98
Reynolds, Freddy, 59
Ribbentrop, Rudolf von, 87
Richard II, 49
Richmond, Duke of, 55
Rigaud, Stephen George, 120, 122
Roberts, boatman, 58
Rockingham, Marquis of, Lord
    Higham Ferrers, 50
Russell, Lord John, 66, 74, **136**
RUTHERFORD, W.G., 62, 76–9,
    80, 102, 118

Sackville, George, 57, 133
Sanger, Ernst, 99
Sankey, Viscount, 90
Sargent, G.R., **48**
SCOTT, C.B., 62, 70, 73–6, 124
Short, Augustus, 62
Sidney, Philip, 28
SMITH, Samuel, 56, 59, 134
Smyth, Charles, 102
Smythe, William, 65, 67
South, Robert, 36, 56, 131
Southey, Robert, 57, **136**
Stanhope, General, 50
Stanhope, Philip, 57, 134
Steele, Richard, 38
Stow, John, 13, 14f.
Stuart, Lynda, 111

Summerscale, D., 142
Swann, Donald, 91, 139
Swift, Jasper, **21**
Swift, Jonathan, 26, 40, 54, 123

Tanner, Lawrence, iv, v, 81–2,
    103, 138
Taswell, Thomas, 43
Thomas, R.J.F., 70
Thynne, John, 75, 124
    Agatha, 122
Tizard, Henry, 80, 104, **138**
Toplady, Augustus, 60, 135
Turle's House, 126, **127**
Tyson, Bursar, 88

UDALL, Nicholas, 19f.
Urquhart, Brian, 83, 139,
Ustinov, Peter, 87, 139
Uvedale, Robert, 37, 131

Vaughans, some time Dorchester
    House, 120
Victoria, Queen, 73
Vincent, Sarah, 37
Vincent Square, **10,** 64, 84, 88, **90,**
    98, 100, 106, 109, 128, 141
Vincent, Tom, 63
VINCENT, William, Dean, 48,
    55f., 61, 71, 102, 128, **134**

Wallis, Albany Charles, 58
Wellington, Duke of, 62
Westminster School Society, 88,
    104
White, Midas, 72
Wickham, Henry, 61
Wilberforce, Samuel, Dean, 66
Willett, A.T., **85**
William IV, 72f., 141
Williams, John, Dean, 28, 33, 119
Williamson, H.S., 86
WILLIAMSON, Richard, 65f., 70,
    72, 137
Williams-Wynn, 71, 116
Wilson, Angus, 83, 138
Wollheim, Richard, 85, 87, 139
Woodville, Elizabeth, 115
Woolf, Virginia, 84f.
Worsley, Pennyman, 67
Wren, Christopher, 46, 119, 131

Yvele, Henry, 114